Eat
Bitch
&
Wine

Just Appetizers

AND WE MEAN BITCH IN A GOOD WAY!

Babe In Total Control of Herself

SOME CALL IT COCKTAIL HOUR,
FOR ME IT'S A SUPPORT GROUP!

TABLE OF CONTENTS

Dips, Spreads & Salsa 1-38

Vegetable Appetizers 39-58

Meat & Poultry Appetizers 59-80

Seafood & Fish Appetizers 81-96

Cheese Appetizers 97-116

Fondue 117-124

Bruchetta, Chips & Bread 125-132

Miscellaneous Appetizers 133-140

Index 141-150

Notes

_____

_____

_____

_____

_____

_____

_____

_____

_____

_____

_____

_____

_____

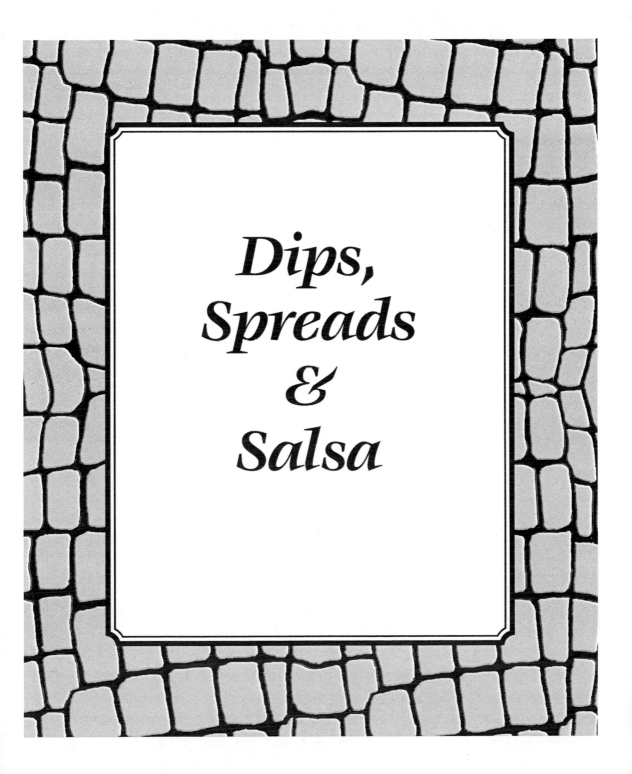

Dips, Spreads & Salsa

MEX-DIP

1/2 lb. ground beef
1-15 1/2 oz. can mashed refried beans
1-8 oz. can tomato sauce
1-1 1/4 oz. pkg. taco seasoning mix
1 small onion, finely chopped
1/2 medium green pepper, finely chopped
1/2 t. dry mustard
1/2 t. chili powder
Sour cream
Finely shredded lettuce
Shredded Cheddar cheese

In a skillet brown the meat and drain. Stir in the next 7 ingredients. Heat to boiling, stirring constantly. Spread into an ungreased pie plate. Spread the topping over the meat mixture. Sprinkle with shredded lettuce and cheese. Makes about 3 1/2 cups.

Topping:
1 C. sour cream
2 T. shredded Cheddar cheese
1/4 t. chili powder

Mix all the ingredients.

TACO DIP SUPREME

Myra Hughes, Drew, MS.

1 lb. or more ground beef
1/2 C. chopped onion
2 tomatoes, chopped
2 avocados, cubed
6 oz. Cheddar cheese, grated
1/2 C. bottled taco sauce
1-8 oz. ctn. sour cream

Preheat oven to 350 degrees F. Brown the onion and ground beef. This can be done in the microwave. Drain. Season with salt and pepper. In a baking pan layer the ground meat, tomatoes and avocados. Fold in taco sauce with the sour cream and spread on top. Top with grated cheese. Bake for 20 minutes until bubbly. Serve with taco chips.

SAUSAGE DIP

1 lb. ground beef
1 lb. pork sausage
1 onion, chopped
2 lbs. Velveeta cheese

1 can Rotel's green chilies and
  tomatoes
1 can mushroom soup
1 t. garlic powder

Brown beef and sausage with the chopped onion. Add the Velveeta cheese. After cheese has melted, add the remaining ingredients. Serve hot with chips.

HOT CRAB DIP

1-8 oz. pkg. cream cheese, softened
1/4 C. mayonnaise
1 t. lemon juice

1/4 C. onion, finely chopped
1 can crabmeat
1/2 C. grated Parmesan cheese

Preheat oven to 375 degrees F. Blend the cream cheese and mayonnaise until smooth. Stir in the remaining ingredients. Spread in a 9-inch pie plate. Bake for 20 minutes. Serve immediately.

*All you need to start an asylum is an empty room
and the right kind of people.*

BLUE CRAB DIP

1-8 oz. pkg. cream cheese, softened
1-6 oz. can lump crabmeat, drained
3 green onions, minced
3 T. heavy whipping cream
3 T. grated Parmesan cheese,
  divided

1 1/2 T. diced red bell pepper
2 t. dry white wine
2 t. chicken soup base
2 t. diced tomatoes
1 t. crab boil seasoning

Fold together all ingredients, except 1 tablespoon Parmesan cheese. Spread evenly in a microwave dish. Microwave on 50% POWER for 4 minutes. Sprinkle with the rest of the Parmesan cheese. Place in the oven and broil until top is browned.

SHRIMP DIP

1/4 lb. butter
1-8 oz. pkg. cream cheese, softened
1/4 C. mayonnaise

2 green onions, finely chopped
1 T. fresh lemon juice
1-4 1/2 oz. can shrimp, drained

Blend all ingredients together.

As you slide down the banister of life, may the splinters never point the wrong way.

ZERBE'S SHRIMP DIP

Pat Zerbe, Duck's General Store, Duck, NC.

2 cans party size shrimp, plus
  juice
2 T. chili sauce

2 t. horseradish
1-8 oz. pkg. cream cheese, cubed
Salt and pepper, to taste

Place the shrimp in a blender and blend slowly. Add the chili sauce, horseradish and cream cheese. Blend. Add the salt and pepper. Serve cold with vegetables or crackers.

SHRIMP LAYERED DIP

Bobbie Williams, Fairview, TX.

2-8 oz. pkg. cream cheese
3/4 C. sour cream
1/2 C. mayonnaise
1 jar cocktail sauce
1 lb. cooked and chopped shrimp

Old Bay seasoning
2 chopped tomatoes
1-8 oz. pkg. Mozzarella cheese,
  grated

Mix the cream cheese, sour cream and mayonnaise. On a large platter, spread the mixture. Layer the next ingredients in the order given. Serve with tortilla chips.

Age is a number and mine is unlisted.

LOUISIANA SHRIMP DIP

1-8 oz. pkg. cream cheese, softened
1-10 3/4 oz. can cream of shrimp
  soup

1/2 t. hot sauce
1/4 C. diced celery
1 1/2 T. diced onion

Mix all the ingredients and chill. Makes 2 1/4 cups.

SHRIMP AND CRAB DIP

1 can shrimp soup
1 roll garlic cheese
2 dashes Worcestershire sauce

1-8 oz. pkg. frozen bits and pieces
  shrimp
1 can crabmeat
Vermouth

In a double boiler, heat the soup and cheese until the cheese melts. Add the rest of the ingredients. Thin with the vermouth if too thick.

A successful man is one who makes more money than his wife can spend.
A successful woman is one who can find such a man.

LOBSTER DIP

1-8 oz. pkg. cream cheese
1/4 C. mayonnaise
1 clove garlic, crushed
1 t. onion, grated
1 t. prepared mustard

1 t. sugar
Season salt, to taste
1-5 oz. can lobster, flaked
3 T. cooking sauterne

Melt the cream cheese over low heat, stirring constantly. Blend in the next 6 ingredients. Stir in the lobster and sauterne. Heat. Serve hot. Makes 1 3/4 cups.

CLAM DIP

1-7 oz. can clams, drained and dried
1/2 C. mayonnaise
1/2 C. sour cream
3 T. lemon juice

2 T. fresh parsley, finely chopped
2 T. scallions, finely chopped
1 t. Worcestershire sauce
Fresh black pepper

Mix the mayonnaise and sour cream until smooth. Stir in the lemon juice, parsley and scallions. Stir in the clams. Mix well. Add the Worcestershire sauce and pepper. Refrigerate.

All men are animals; some just make better pets!

SMOKED SALMON AND DILL DIP

8 oz. smoked salmon pieces
1-8 oz. pkg. cream cheese, softened
Grated peel of 1 small lemon
1 T. lemon juice

1 C. heavy cream
3 T. chopped fresh dill
2 scallions, finely chopped
Fresh black pepper

Add the first 4 ingredients to a food processor. Process until smooth. With machine running, gradually pour in cream until mixture is soft. Add the rest of the ingredients and process to blend. Place in bowl and cover. Refrigerate until ready to serve.

CHICKEN ENCHILADA DIP

Pat Snyder, Dallas, TX.

2-3 chicken breasts, roasted and
  chopped
2-8 oz. pkg. light cream cheese,
  room temperature
1 1/3 C. Cheddar cheese, grated
2 garlic cloves, minced
1 1/2 T. chili powder
1 t. cumin powder
1 t. dry oregano

1 t. paprika
Cayenne pepper, to taste
Tabasco, to taste
1 bunch cilantro, chopped
4 green onions, chopped
1 can diced tomatoes, do not drain
1-4 oz. can diced green chilies, do
  not drain

Mix the cheeses until well blended. Add the next 7 ingredients. Mix well. In another bowl, add the chicken and the rest of the ingredients. Fold into the cheese mixture. Refrigerate overnight or 8 hours. Heat and serve. Makes a ton.

REUBEN DIP

1-8 oz. pkg. cream cheese, softened
8 oz. shredded Swiss cheese
1 can sauerkraut, drained

14 oz. shaved corned beef, cut into
 1/2-inch strips
8 T. thousand island dressing

Preheat oven to 375 degrees F. Mix all the ingredients, except the dressing. Pour into a 9-inch square casserole dish and drizzle with the dressing. Bake for 20 to 30 minutes. Serve warm.

B.L.T. DIP

1 lb. bacon, fried and drained
1 C. mayonnaise
1 C. sour cream

1 tomato, diced
Shredded lettuce

Combine the mayonnaise and sour cream. Crumble bacon into the mixture. Mix in tomatoes and sprinkle with shredded lettuce. Serve with toasted bread.

A southern lady doesn't need a man to make her happy....
but a maid is essential.

CURRY DIP FOR RAW VEGETABLES

1 C. mayonnaise
1/4 tsp. horseradish
1/4 C. buttermilk
Dash of Tabasco sauce

1 t. curry powder
Dash of red pepper
1/4 tsp. onion powder
Salt and pepper, to taste

Combine all ingredients. Refrigerate and surround by raw vegetables.

SUN-DRIED TOMATO BASIL DIP

1 T. pine nuts
3 oz. sun-dried tomatoes in olive oil
4 oz. cream cheese
1/2 C. mayonnaise

2 cloves garlic, crushed
1 T. balsamic vinegar
3 T. oil from sun-dried tomato
1 T. chopped fresh oregano
2 T. fresh basil, torn into pieces

Toast the pine nuts for 5 minutes. Coarsely chop sun-fried tomatoes. Put in a food processor. Add the cream cheese, mayonnaise, garlic, vinegar and oil. Process until nearly smooth. Add the oregano and basil and process until smooth. Refrigerate about 15 minutes. Sprinkle with pine nuts.

Are my hot flashes causing global warming?

7 LAYER DIP

1 can bean dip
1 can refried beans
1-8 oz. pkg. cream cheese, softened
3 T. picante sauce
Guacamole

8 oz. Colby-Jack cheese, grated
1 tomato, diced
1 green onion, diced
1 small can black olives, chopped

Layer ingredients in the order listed.

GARBANZO DIP

1-19 oz. can garbanzo beans,
  drained
1/2 C. oil-free Italian dressing

1 T. fresh lemon juice
1 clove garlic

Combine all the ingredients in a food processor. Blend until smooth. Chill. Makes 1 1/3 cups.

At my age, getting lucky means finding my car in the parking lot.

BLACK BEAN NACHO DIP

1 onion, chopped
2 garlic cloves, chopped
2 T. olive oil
2 T. chili powder
2-15 oz. cans black beans
1 t. cumin seed
Cayenne pepper, to taste

10 oz. Monterey Jack cheese, grated
Salt, to taste
2 tomatoes, chopped
3 T. chopped fresh cilantro
2 T. jalapeño pepper
1 C. sour cream

Preheat oven to 450 degrees F. Spray a casserole dish with Pam. In a medium saucepan, sauté the onion and garlic in the oil until clear. Sprinkle with chili powder and cook 1 minute longer. Add 1 can of drained beans and 1 can of undrained beans. Cook until the mixture thickens. Mash the beans until the mixture is half smooth and half chunky. Add the cumin seeds. Season with the salt and cayenne. Spoon the mixture into the casserole dish and top with cheese. Bake for 10 minutes, or until cheese is melted. Remove from the oven and spread the casserole with sour cream. Top with the tomatoes, cilantro and jalapeño pepper.

RASPBERRY CHIPOTLE BLACK BEAN DIP

Pat Snyder, Dallas, TX.

3 C. black beans, drained and mashed
1 red onion, chopped
3 cloves garlic, pressed
1-8 oz. pkg. cream cheese

3/4 jar raspberry chipotle sauce
1 pkg. grated Monterey Jack cheese
1 T. salt
1 T. Creole seasoning

Preheat oven to 350 degrees F. Spray Pam in a 7x11-inch baking dish. Combine the beans, onion, garlic and seasonings. Spread in the baking dish. Crumble the cream cheese and pour the sauce on top. Top with the cheese. Bake 20 to 25 minutes, until the cheese is melted. Serve with chips.

BLACK BEAN DIP

1 medium onion, finely chopped
2 t. olive oil
2 cloves garlic, minced
2-15 oz. cans black beans, rinsed
   and drained
1 T. lime juice

2 T. white vinegar
1 t. coriander
1 t. cumin
1 jalapeño chili, seeded and
   chopped
Black pepper, to taste

Sauté the onion in the oil until the onion softens. Add the garlic and cook for 30 seconds. Add these and the rest of the ingredients to a food processor and process until smooth. Refrigerate. Makes 2 1/2 cups.

THREE-CHEESE BAKED ARTICHOKE DIP

2 bags pita bread
2-6 oz. jars marinated artichoke
   hearts, drained
1/2 onion, finely chopped
3 cloves garlic, minced

3 C. Mozzarella cheese, shredded
1-8 oz. pkg. cream cheese, softened
1 C. grated Parmesan cheese
1 C. mayonnaise

Preheat oven to 350 degrees F. Cut pita bread in to chip-size triangles and separate in 2 pieces each. Place on a baking sheet and bake for 5 to 7 minutes, or until crispy. In a food processor, add the artichokes, onion and garlic. Process until chopped. Place in a large bowl and stir in the cheeses and mayonnaise. Spoon into a lightly greased 2-quart baking dish. Bake for 30 minutes. Serve with the pita chips. Makes 12 to 16 servings.

KING ARTICHOKE DIP

8 slices bacon, cut into small
  pieces
1 C. finely-chopped onion
2 cloves garlic, minced
1-14 oz. can artichoke hearts,
  drained and chopped

1-8 oz. pkg. cream cheese, softened
1/2 C. sour cream
3 C. chopped fresh spinach
1/4 t. Worcestershire sauce

Sauté the bacon, onion and garlic. Add the artichoke and sauté 1 minute more. Beat cream cheese and sour cream in bowl until smooth. Add bacon mixture. Stir. Mix in spinach and Worcestershire sauce. Serve in a hollowed out loaf with bread chunks for dipping. Makes 3 cups.

BROCCOLI DIP

1 pkg. chopped broccoli
1/2 t. salt
1/4 C. water
1 onion, chopped
3/4 C. slivered almonds

2 T. margarine
1 can cream of mushroom soup
1 roll garlic cheese
1/8 t. Tabasco sauce

Cook broccoli in the salt and water. Drain. Sauté onion in the margarine. Add the rest of the ingredients, except the broccoli, and simmer until cheese is melted. Add the broccoli and cook 1 minute. Serve hot.

A friend knows your faults, but loves you anyway.

ASPARAGUS DIP

1 lb. asparagus
1 tomato, chopped
2 T. onion, chopped
2 T. lemon juice
1 clove garlic, chopped

1 t. cumin
1 t. chili powder
1/2 t. salt
Dash of hot sauce
1/2 C. sour cream

Cook asparagus until very tender. Drain and rinse under cold water. Pat dry. Chop into large pieces. Place in a food processor. Add the rest of the ingredients, except sour cream and blend. Add the sour cream and whirl briefly to blend. Refrigerate for 2 hours before serving.

MEXICAN CORN DIP

Carolyn Raney, El Dorado, AR.

3 cans Mexican corn, drained
6 green onions, chopped
1 C. mayonnaise
Cilantro, to taste
Garlic, to taste

1-4 oz. can chopped green chilies
1-10 oz. pkg. Cheddar cheese,
  grated
1 C. sour cream
Cumin, to taste

Mix all ingredients and chill. Serves 20.

A new pair of shoes can change your life.

AVOCADO LIME DIP

2 avocados, peeled and seed
  removed
1 C. nonfat plain yogurt

1/4 C. lime juice
2 cloves garlic
1 t. salt

Place all ingredients in a food processor and blend until all is smooth.

ROASTED ONION GUACAMOLE DIP

1 large purple onion, chopped
2 garlic cloves, chopped
2 T. balsamic vinegar
1 T. olive oil
4 small avocados

1 T. lemon juice
1/2 t. salt
1/2 t. dried Italian seasoning
Tortilla chips

Preheat oven to 425 degrees F. Toss together the first 4 ingredients and place in a foil lined pan. Bake for 25 to 30 minutes, stirring mixture once. Cool. Peel and mash the avocados. Stir in the onion mixture and the rest of the ingredients, except the chips. Chill 1 hour. Makes 2 cups.

Behind every successful woman is herself.

HORSERADISH DIP

1/3 C. chili sauce

1 C. sour cream

1 T. horseradish

1 t. Worcestershire sauce

Stir the chili sauce into the sour cream. Mix in the rest of the ingredients. Chill.

VEGETABLE DIP

2 C. mayonnaise

1/2 C. chopped onion

1-6 oz. pkg. cream cheese

2 t. Worcestershire sauce

Place in a blender. Serve with raw vegetables.

Chablis makes me think naughty things; merlot makes me say them, champagne makes me do them.

CUCUMBER DIP

1/2 qt. yogurt
3 garlic cloves
1/2 C. olive oil

1/2 cucumber, peeled and diced in
small pieces

Place the garlic through a garlic press, and add to the yogurt in a bowl. Add the cucumbers. Slowly mix the oil with a fork. Add a few drops on top. Chill. Serve with pita bread cut into quarters.

ROASTED EGGPLANT DIP

2 medium eggplants
1/4 C. fresh lemon juice
1/4 C. extra-virgin olive oil
1/2 t. minced garlic

1/2 C. freshly-grated Parmesan
cheese
Salt and pepper, to taste

Preheat oven to 500 degrees F. Pierce the eggplant in several places and cook for 15 to 30 minutes until the skin blackens. Remove and cool. Part the skin and scoop out the flesh and mince it finely. Mix it with the rest of the ingredients. Makes 6 servings.

Be nice to your children, they choose your nursing home.

SPINACH ARTICHOKE SALSA DIP

2-8 oz. pkg. cream cheese, softened
3/4 C. heavy cream
1/3 C. Parmesan cheese, grated
1/4 t. garlic powder
1 bunch fresh spinach, chopped,
  or 1-16 oz. pkg. frozen cut leaf
  spinach, thawed and drained

1-13 oz. can marinated artichoke
  hearts, drained and chopped
2/3 C. shredded Monterey Jack
  cheese
1 C. Mexican salsa of your choice

Preheat the oven to 300 degrees F. Blend the cream cheese and cream with a hand mixer. Add the garlic and cheeses and mix until smooth and creamy. Fold in the spinach and artichokes. Place in a casserole dish and bake for 1 hour. Remove from the oven, and spoon the salsas around the outer edge. Return to the oven for 15 minutes.

SOUTHERN CAVIAR DIP

4 C. frozen or canned black-eyed
  peas
1-16 oz. can white hominy, drained
2 tomatoes, chopped
1 C. Italian dressing
1 C. chopped green pepper
1/2 C. chopped onion

4 scallions, sliced
2 jalapeño peppers, seeded and
  chopped
2 cloves garlic, minced
1/4 C. sour cream
Cilantro, chopped

Cook the frozen peas according to directions. In a large bowl, add all the ingredients, except the sour cream. Cover and chill for 1 or 2 days. Drain the mixture, reserving the liquid. Place in a blender and pulse twice. Add enough of the juice for dipping consistency. Top with the sour cream and cilantro. Makes 10 cups.

SANDY'S MUSHROOM SPREAD

Virginia Truitt, Sassy Selections, Martinsville, VA.

1 lb. fresh mushrooms, finely
  chopped
2 T. butter

2 egg yolks, beaten
Salt
1 recipe cream cheese with onion

Cream Cheese with Onion:
2-3 oz. pkg. cream cheese, softened
4 green onions, minced
2 T. butter

2 T. white wine
1/4 C. sour cream

Sauté mushrooms in the butter and drain. Combine with cream cheese with onion recipe. Beat in the egg yolks. Do this in a skillet. Season with salt. To make the cream cheese with onion recipe, sauté the onions in the butter and wine until the liquid is evaporated. Add the cream cheese and sour cream. Blend thoroughly. Can be frozen. Thaw in top of a double boiler. Triple this recipe if putting into a chaffing dish.

SMOKY EGG DIP

6 hard-boiled eggs, mashed
1/3 C. mayonnaise
1 T. butter, softened
1/2 t. salt
2 t. prepared mustard
1 1/2 t. lemon juice

1 1/2 t. Worcestershire sauce
1/8 t. liquid smoke
2 drops hot pepper sauce
Dash of pepper
4 slices crisp cooked bacon,
  crumbled

Add all the ingredients, except the bacon and mix well. Chill. When ready to serve, add the bacon and mix well.

SPICY PEANUT DIP

1 T. vegetable oil
1 shallot, chopped
1 T. fresh ginger, minced
2 garlic clove, minced
1 t. curry powder
1/8 t. dried crushed red pepper

1 C. canned low-salt chicken broth
1/2 C. creamy peanut butter
4 t. fresh lime juice
1 T. soy sauce
1 t. brown sugar

Heat the oil in a skillet over medium heat. Add the next 3 ingredients and sauté for 3 minutes. Add the curry and red pepper and cook for 15 seconds. Stir in the rest of the ingredients. Simmer about 3 minutes until mixture thickens. Place in a bowl and cool. Cover and refrigerate for 2 hours. It can be refrigerated up to 2 days. Makes 1 1/3 cups.

HOT PECAN DIP

3/4 C. chopped pecans
2 T. butter, melted
1/2 t. salt
1-8 oz. pkg. cream cheese, softened
2 T. milk
2 1/2 oz. dried beef, chopped

1/4 C. green pepper, finely
  chopped
1/2 small onion, grated
1/2 t. garlic powder
Pepper, to taste
1/2 C. sour cream

Preheat oven to 350 degrees F. Combine the pecans, butter and salt. Spread out in a pie plate. Bake 15 minutes. Cool. Combine remaining ingredients in given order. Pour into an ungreased, shallow 8- to 9-inch baking dish. Cover with the pecan mixture. Bake 20 minutes.

CHIPOTLE MAYONNAISE DIP WITH CARROTS

1 C. mayonnaise
1 C. sour cream

2 canned chipotle chilies in adobo
    sauce, mince the chilies to 1 T.
    paste, plus 1/2 t. adobo sauce
Carrots

In a bowl, whisk all ingredients, except carrots. Refrigerate. Serve carrots with the dip.

BLUE CHEESE AND CARAMELIZED SHALLOT DIP

1 T. vegetable oil
1 1/4 C. thinly-sliced shallots
3/4 C. mayonnaise

3/4 C. sour cream
4 oz. blue cheese, room
    temperature

In a medium saucepan, heat the oil over medium-low heat. Add the shallots. Cover and cook until shallots are deep golden brown, stirring occasionally, about 20 minutes. Cool. Whisk together the mayonnaise and sour cream in a bowl to blend. Add the cheese. Using a rubber spatula, mash mixture and smooth. Stir in the shallots. Cover and refrigerate for at least 2 hours. Makes 2 cups.

Better to have loved and lost than to have
spent your entire life with a psycho.

LAYERED PIZZA DIP

8 oz. reduced-fat free cream
 cheese, softened
1/2 C. chunky pizza sauce
1/4 C. green bell pepper, chopped

1/3 C. sliced mushrooms
1/4 C. minced onion
1 C. reduced-fat shredded
 Cheddar cheese

Preheat oven to 350 degrees F. Layer all the ingredients in the order given, starting by spreading cream cheese evenly over the bottom of a pie pan. Bake for 15 minutes.

WHITE CHEESE DIP

6 C. shredded Asadero cheese
1 onion, chopped fine
1 t. Tabasco sauce
3 jalapeño peppers, seeded and
 chopped fine

2 T. prepared horseradish
2 cloves garlic, chopped fine
1 C. beer

Combine in a crock pot and stir. Cook over low heat until cheese is melted.

By the time I got to greener pastures, I couldn't climb the fences.

MEDITERRANEAN FETA DIP

1 pkg. Knorr vegetable soup mix
1-16 oz. ctn. sour cream
1/2 cucumber, peeled, seeded and
  diced

4 oz. Feta cheese, crumbled
2 T. chopped red onion
1/2 t. oregano

Mix all the ingredients and mix well. Chill for at least 2 hours.

CHEESE WREATH

2-8 oz. pkg. cream cheese, softened
1-8 oz. sharp Cheddar cheese,
  shredded
1 T. chopped red bell pepper

1 T. finely-chopped onion
2 t. Worcestershire sauce
1 t. lemon juice
Dash of ground red pepper

Mix the cream cheese and Cheddar cheese with an electric mixer on medium speed until well blended. Blend in rest of the ingredients. Refrigerate overnight. When ready to serve, place a drinking glass in the center of a serving platter. Drop round tablespoonfuls of cheese mixture around the glass. Touch the outer edge of the glass to form the ring. Smooth with a spatula to create a wreath. Remove the glass. Garnish with chopped fresh parsley and additional chopped red bell pepper.

Before I share a man's company, I make sure he owns it.

QUICK FRUIT DIP

1-8 oz. pkg. cream cheese, softened   1 C. orange juice
1-16 oz. ctn. Cool Whip

Combine all the ingredients in a blender and blend until smooth. Chill before serving.

FRUIT WITH LIME DIP

2 C. strawberries
1 large papaya, seeded and cut
  into chunks

1/2 fresh pineapple, cut into
  chunks

Dip:
1 C. whipping cream, whipped
3 T. powdered sugar
1 t. vanilla extract

2 t. grated lime peel
1 egg white

Four hours before serving, cover and refrigerate the fruit. Also, mix the next 4 ingredients and refrigerate. Before serving, beat the egg white until peaks form. Fold the cream mixture into the egg white. Use wooden toothpicks to dip the fruit into the dip. Makes 2 1/2 cups.

Both of us can't look good at the same time, it's either me or the house!

MAPLE SYRUP DIP

1 C. sour cream   1/2 C. real maple syrup
1 C. whipped cream

Mix together and place in refrigerator for 4 hours and serve with fruit platter.

RUM FRUIT DIP

3.4 oz. instant vanilla pudding   1 T. sugar
2 1/2 C. half & half   1 t. vanilla flavoring
1 t. rum flavoring

Mix all ingredients with mixer for 2 minutes. Chill for several hours or overnight. Arrange fruit pieces around dip.

Born to shop; forced to cook!

COFFEE FRUIT DIP

1-8 oz. pkg. cream cheese, softened
1-8 oz. ctn. sour cream
1/2 C. brown sugar

1/3 C. coffee-flavored liqueur
1-8 oz. ctn. frozen whipped
   topping, thawed

Beat all ingredients, except whipped topping, with an electric mixer until smooth. Fold in the topping. Chill until serving.

FRUIT DIP

1-8 oz. pkg. cream cheese, softened
1/2 C. sour cream
1 C. whipped cream
1/4 C. brown sugar

1/4 C. sugar
1 T. maple syrup
1 t. vanilla

Combine all ingredients and mix until smooth. Chill before serving.

Coffee is cheaper than Prozac.

MARSHMALLOW CREAM DIP

1-8 oz. pkg. cream cheese, softened   1 T. maraschino cherry juice
16 oz. marshmallow creme

Place cream cheese and marshmallow creme in a microwave-safe bowl.
Place in microwave and cook on MEDIUM-HIGH for 20 second increments,
until softened. Stir cherry juice into the cream cheese and marshmallow
creme mixture. Cover and refrigerate until chilled. Serves 12.

YOGURT DIP

2 C. yogurt   1/2 t. dried mint, crumbled, or 1 t.
1 clove garlic, minced   fresh, chopped
1/2 cucumber, seeded and chopped
   fine

Mix all the ingredients and chill thoroughly. Makes 2 cups.

Can it be a mistake that "stressed" is "desserts" backwards?

SHRIMP MESS

5 lb. large shrimp, cooked
1 C. oil
1/2 C. ketchup
1 T. Worcestershire sauce

1 jar horseradish
1 jar brown mustard
1 large onion, in rings
1/4 C. vinegar

Mix all the ingredients and mix well. Heavily salt and pepper. Marinate and refrigerate overnight.

HOT SEAFOOD SPREAD

1-8 oz. pkg. cream cheese, softened
8 oz. shredded Cheddar cheese
1 C. mayonnaise
1 can tiny shrimp, rinsed and
  drained
1 can crabmeat

1/2 C. green onion, chopped
1/4 C. Parmesan cheese, grated
2 t. dill weed
2 t. fresh parsley, minced
1 round loaf unsliced bread

Preheat oven to 350 degrees F. Mix first 9 ingredients. Hollow out bread leaving 1/2-inch shell. Fill bread with seafood mixture. Place on an ungreased cookie sheet and cover loosely with foil. Bake for 25 minutes. Remove foil and bake for 25 minutes more. Serve with veggies or corn chips.

Chocolate makes your clothes shrink!

CRABMEAT SPREAD

1-12 oz. pkg. cream cheese,
  softened
1 T. Worcestershire sauce
1 T. lemon juice
2 T. mayonnaise

1 small onion, grated
Pinch of garlic salt
1/2 lb. cooked crabmeat, flaked
6 oz. chili sauce

Mix all the ingredients, except the chili sauce. Mix well. Spread in a shallow serving dish. Pour the chili sauce over the crab mixture. Refrigerate for at least 2 hours. Serve with crackers. Serves 15.

HUMMUS

Terry Saba, Chandler, AZ.

1 can garbanzo beans, drained
3 T. tahini (sesame paste)
1/4 C. lemon juice

1/2 C. bean juice
1 garlic clove, pressed
Salt, to taste

Combine in food processor or blender. Garnish with olive oil and paprika. Serve with pita wedges. For variation, add one of the following: dill, jalapeño or peeled puréed roasted red pepper. May be frozen up to three months.

Dear Lord, if you can't make me skinny, please make my friends fat.

OLIVE SPREAD WITH WALNUTS

1 3/4 C. pitted Kalamata olives,
  finely chopped
3 T. + 1/4 C. walnuts, toasted and
  chopped
1/4 C. olive oil
2 t. Dijon mustard

1 garlic clove
1 t. fresh thyme, chopped
1 t. fresh oregano, chopped
1 t. fresh sage, chopped
Cayenne pepper, to taste

In a food processor, add the olives, 3 tablespoons walnuts and the rest of the ingredients. Process until coarsely puréed. Stir in the remaining 1/4 cup chopped walnuts. Makes 1 1/2 cups.

SALMON TARTAR SPREAD

1/4 C. capers, packed in brine and
  drain
1-8 oz. smoked salmon
2 T. fresh dill, chopped

2 T. extra-virgin olive oil
1/2 t. finely-grated lemon zest
1/4 C. red onion, finely diced

In a food processor, pulse the capers until coarsely chopped. Add the salmon, dill, olive oil and lemon zest and pulse until salmon is finely chopped and well mixed. Stir in the red onion.

Dull women have immaculate homes.

ROASTED EGGPLANT AND PESTO SPREAD

1 large eggplant
1/4 C. pesto
1 large lemon

Kosher salt
Black pepper

Place the eggplant on a baking sheet and broil cook for a few minutes, turning several times so the skin blisters and chars. Preheat oven to 400 degrees F. Keep the eggplant on the baking sheet and bake for 50 minutes, turning once. Remove and cut eggplant in half length-wise and let cool for 10 minutes. Scoop out flesh and place in a bowl of a food processor. Add pesto and grate lemon to get 1/2 teaspoon zest. Cut lemon in half and squeeze 2 tablespoons juice in the processor. Process until fairly smooth. Place in a bowl and add the salt and pepper. Cover and refrigerate until cold. Makes 1 2/3 cups.

NACHO CHICKEN SPREAD

1-4 oz. shredded mild Cheddar or
  Monterey Jack cheese
1 C. shredded cooked chicken
1 C. sour cream

1 T. pkg. taco seasoning mix
1/2 C. canned corn, drained
1-4 oz. can chopped green chilies
Chopped jalapeño, to taste

Mix all the ingredients and refrigerate for at least 1 hour before serving.

Drink 'till he's cute!

VERY GOUDA SPREAD

1-8 oz. round Gouda cheese
1 T. milk
1 T. dry white wine or apple juice

1 t. prepared mustard
2 drops red pepper sauce

Let cheese stand at room temperature until softened. Make four 2 1/2-inch intersecting cuts in top of cheese ball, cutting completely through plastic casing. Carefully pull back each section of casing, curling point over index finger. Scoop out cheese, leaving 1/4-inch wall. Refrigerate casing shell. Mash cheese with fork. Mix in remaining ingredients. Fill casing shell with cheese mixture. Cover and refrigerate until firm, about 3 hours. Let stand at room temperature 1 hour before serving. Garnish with parsley, if desired. Accompany with crackers.

JALAPEÑO CHEESE SPREAD

1 small onion, quartered
2 fresh jalapeños, seeded
2-3 oz. pkg. cream cheese
Juice of 1 lemon
1 T. Worcestershire sauce
4 oz. sharp Cheddar cheese, grated

4 oz. longhorn Cheddar cheese,
  grated
4 oz. pimento cheese spread
1/4 C. chopped pecans
1 t. paprika
Parsley

Finely chop the onion and jalapeños in a food processor. Add the cream cheese, lemon juice and Worcestershire sauce. Process until well blended. In a medium bowl, combine the cheeses, pecans and paprika. Stir until thoroughly blended. Add the jalapeño mixture. Mix well. Shape on a serving plate. Garnish with parsley. Serve with crackers or chips. Makes 3 cups.

CHEESE SPREAD

Janie Hamilton, Treasure Seekers, Charlotte, NC.

1 small ctn. pimento cheese (Mrs. Weaver or Grisom-no pickles)
1/4 lb. shredded sharp Cheddar cheese
2-3 oz. pkg. Philadelphia cream cheese
1/2 t. salt
1/2 t. cayenne pepper
3 T. Worcestershire sauce
1 t. chopped onion
1 C. finely-chopped pecans

In a blender, mix the first 7 ingredients. Mix thoroughly. Add pecans and mix to blend only. Put into serving bowl and refrigerate. Take out 30 minutes before serving.

SEAFOOD SALSA

3 green onions, dried
1/4 C. diced red onion
1/2 t. minced garlic
2 jalapeño peppers, cored, seeded and diced
3 tomatoes, cored, diced and drained
1/2 C. finely-chopped fresh cilantro
1 t. dried oregano
1/4 t. ground cumin
1 T. fresh lime juice
1/4 lb. small shrimp, cooked and peeled
1/4 lb. bay scallops, cooked
1 avocado, peeled, seeded and diced
1 C. fresh or frozen corn kernels
Salt
Garnish: lime wedges and fresh cilantro leaves

In food processor, combine green onions, red onion, garlic, jalapeños, tomatoes, cilantro, oregano, cumin and lime juice. Pulse about 4 times and set aside. In large glass bowl, combine shrimp, scallops, avocado and corn. Add reserved onion mixture and toss to blend. Season with salt to taste. Cover and chill 1 to 2 hours. Garnish with lime wedges and cilantro. Serve with tortilla chips or drain and place over fresh endive for a first course. Makes 4 to 6 cups.

ARTICHOKE SALSA

1-6.5 oz. jar marinated artichoke
  hearts, drained and chopped
3 roma tomatoes, chopped
2 T. chopped red onions

1/4 C. chopped black olives
1 T. chopped garlic
2 T. chopped fresh basil
Salt and pepper, to taste

Mix all ingredients. Serve chilled or at room temperature. Makes 1 1/4 cups.

CORN AND TOMATO SALSA

1 C. fresh corn kernels, 2 small
  ears
1 large tomato, seeded and
  chopped
2/3 C. chopped red onion
1/2 C. chopped fresh cilantro
2 T. olive oil

1 T. fresh lemon juice
1/2 t. ground cumin
1 jalapeño chili, seeded and
  minced
1 avocado, pitted, peeled and
  chopped
Fresh cilantro sprigs

Mix all ingredients. Cover and chill before serving.

Eat, drink and re-marry.

MARGARITA JALAPEÑO SALSA

Larry Wright, L.L. Wright Showroom, Overland Park, KS

1 C. cubed tomato
1/2 C. medium-fine chopped white
   or red onion
4 fresh jalapeños, very finely
   minced

1 clove garlic, minced
1/4 t. salt
1/4 C. gold or white tequila

Combine all ingredients and let stand at room temperature for 30 minutes. Makes about 1 1/2 cups.

TROPICAL FRUIT SALSA

1 mango, peeled and cut into
   cubes
1 papaya, peeled and cut into
   cubes
1 avocado, peeled and cut into
   cubes

3 T. lime juice
2 T. fresh cilantro, chopped
2 T. brown sugar
1 t. jalapeño pepper, drained
1 t. ginger, crushed

Combine all ingredients in a bowl. Cover and refrigerate at least 1 hour.

Ever feel like a Raggedy Ann in a Barbie doll world?

STRAWBERRY SALSA

1/2 medium red onion, thinly sliced

1 jalapeño pepper, minced

1/2 red bell pepper, stemmed, seeded and julienned

1/2 green bell pepper, stemmed, seeded and julienned

1/4 C. finely-shredded fresh cilantro leaves

1 C. fresh strawberries, hulled and sliced

1/4 C. fresh orange juice

2 T. fresh lime juice

2 T. extra-virgin olive oil

Salt and pepper, to taste

Place all ingredients in a large bowl and toss. Cover and refrigerate at least 2 hours. Remove 15 minutes before serving. Makes 2 1/2 cups.

CRANBERRY SALSA

1 1/2 C. fresh cranberries, coarsely chopped*

1/3 C. sugar

1/4 C. green onion, sliced

1/4 C. fresh cilantro, chopped

Juice of 1 lime

Grated zest of the lime

1 jalapeño chili, seeded and minced

2 t. ginger root, finely chopped

1/2 t. salt

Mix all ingredients; cover and chill. This is great with turkey. Makes 1 1/2 cups.

*Use frozen if you cannot find fresh.

CRANBERRY-PINEAPPLE SALSA

1-12 oz. bag fresh cranberries
1/4 C. granulated sugar
1 scallion, white and green parts,
   coarsely chopped
1 garlic clove, minced

1/2 medium pineapple, pared,
   cored and coarsely chopped,
   about 2 packed cups
2 T. chopped fresh mint or cilantro
1 or 2 jalapeños, seeded and
   minced, or to taste
1/4 t. salt

Place all the ingredients in a food processor fitted with the metal blade. Pulse until the cranberries are coarsely chopped. Transfer to a serving dish and cover tightly with plastic wrap. Refrigerate for at least 30 minutes, but no longer than 2 hours. Serve chilled. Makes about 3 1/2 cups.

CORN SALSA

2-17 oz. cans whole kernel corn,
   rinsed and drained
1-4 oz. can chopped green chilies,
   drained
1-2 1/2 oz. can sliced pitted ripe
   olives, drained
1 large tomato, chopped

2 to 3 jalapeño peppers, seeded
   and finely chopped
3 T. white vinegar
1/3 C. olive oil or vegetable oil
1/2 t. salt
1 T. chopped fresh cilantro

Combine first 8 ingredients in a non-aluminum bowl; add cilantro, if desired. Cover and chill at least 2 hours, stirring often. Serve with tortilla chips or as a relish with grilled beef or chicken. Makes 6 cups.

BLACK-EYED PEA SALSA

2 medium tomatoes, seeded and
  chopped
1-15 oz. can black-eyed peas,
  rinsed and drained
1 medium green pepper, chopped
1/2 C. sliced green onion
1/2 C. snipped fresh cilantro
  leaves

2 T. lemon juice
1 jalapeño pepper, seeded and
  finely chopped
2 cloves garlic, minced
1/4 t. ground cumin, divided
1/2 t. salt
1 t. garlic powder

Combine all ingredients and mix well. Cover and chill at least 4 hours.
Serve with chips.

If I keel over in Wal-Mart, drag my body to Neiman's!

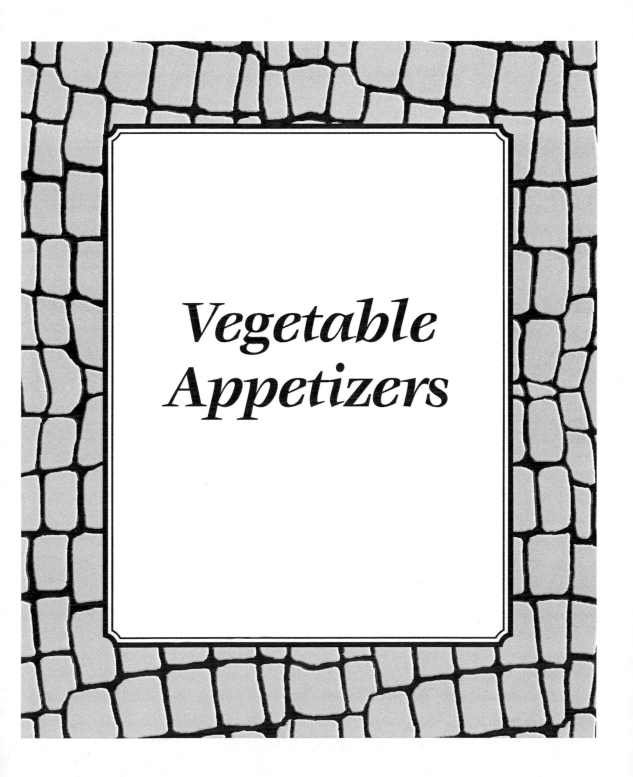

Vegetable
Appetizers

ARTICHOKE NIBBLES

2-6 oz. jars marinated artichoke
   hearts
1 small onion, finely chopped
1 clove garlic, minced
4 eggs
1/4 C. fine, dry bread crumbs

1/4 t. salt
1/8 t. each pepper, oregano leaves
   and liquid hot pepper seasoning
2 C. shredded sharp Cheddar
   cheese
2 T. minced parsley

Preheat oven to 325 degrees F. Drain 1 jar of the artichokes into a skillet. Drain the other jar. Chop all the artichokes. Set aside. Heat the juice over medium heat. Add the onion and garlic and cook, stirring until onion is soft. Beat the egg and stir in the bread crumbs and all the seasonings. Add the artichokes and onions. Mix well. Bake in a greased 7x11-inch baking pan. Bake for 30 minutes. Let cool slightly. Cut into 1-inch squares. Serve warm. Makes 6 dozen.

ARTICHOKE CHEESE SQUARES

1/4 C. onion, chopped
1 clove garlic, mashed
3 T. bacon fat
4 eggs, beaten until frothy
1-14 oz. jar artichoke hearts,
   drained and chopped
1/2 lb. Swiss cheese, grated

2 T. parsley, minced
1/2 t. salt
1/4 t. oregano
1/4 t. Tabasco sauce
1/2 C. dry unseasoned bread
   crumbs

In a frying pan, sauté onions and garlic in bacon fat. Add the remaining ingredients and mix well. Pour into a greased 7x11-inch baking dish. Bake in a preheated 325 degrees F. oven for 25 to 30 minutes. Cut into 1-inch squares. Makes 77 squares.

ARTICHOKE CHEESECAKE

4 T. unsalted butter, melted
8 sheets frozen phyllo dough, thawed
3 oz. marinated artichoke hearts
3-8 oz. pkg. cream cheese, softened
5 oz. Feta cheese, crumbled

1 1/2 t. fresh oregano, chopped
1/2 t. garlic powder
3 large eggs
1/4 C. green onions, chopped
Roma tomatoes, sliced
Greek olives, pitted

Preheat oven to 400 degrees F. Brush bottom and sides of a 9-inch springform pan with butter. Place 1 sheet of phyllo in the pan so that it extends over the sides of the pan. Brush with butter. Repeat with the remaining phyllo and butter. Make 2 slits in the center of the phyllo. Bake 9 to 10 minutes. Cool on a wire rack. Decrease oven temperature to 325 degrees F. Drain and chop the artichokes, reserving 2 tablespoons of the juice. Set aside. Beat the cream cheese, Feta, oregano and garlic powder in a large bowl. Add eggs, beating just until blended. Do not overbeat. Add artichoke hearts, juice and green onions. Mix well. Pour into the crust and cover loosely with foil. Bake 35 to 40 minutes. Cool. Cover and chill 2 hours or up to 24 hours. When ready to serve, remove from pan and garnish with the tomatoes and olives. Serves 14.

Every time I find Mr. Right my husband scares him off!

ARTICHOKE FRITTATA

2-6 oz. jars marinated artichoke
  hearts
1 onion, peeled and chopped
1 T. minced garlic
6 large eggs
1/4 C. fine dried bread crumbs

1/2 t. hot sauce
1/4 t. salt
1/4 t. pepper
1/4 t. dried oregano
2 C. shredded Cheddar cheese
1/4 C. shredded Parmesan cheese

Preheat the oven to 350 degrees F. Drain the hearts, saving 2 tablespoons of the juice. Coarsely chop the artichoke hearts. In a skillet, add the liquid, onion and garlic. Cook until the onion is limp. In a large bowl, whisk the eggs, crumbs, hot sauce, salt, pepper, oregano and Cheddar cheese. Stir in the artichokes. Pour into the onion mixture. Sprinkle Parmesan cheese over the top. Bake in oven for 30 minutes. Serve warm. Cut into 12 wedges.

ITALIAN-STYLE QUESADILLAS

10-8 oz. flour tortillas
6 oz. blue cheese, softened
12 oz. sliced Provolone cheese

1-7 oz. jar roasted red peppers
1-8 1/2 oz. can artichoke hearts,
  drained and chopped

Preheat oven to 400 degrees F. Place 5 tortillas and spread with a thin layer of the blue cheese, leaving a 1/2-inch border all around. Cover each with 2 slices of Provolone. Sprinkle about 1 tablespoon red peppers and 1 tablespoon artichokes over the cheese. Top each with a tortilla. Heat a skillet over high heat until hot. Reduce the heat to medium. Cook quesadilla about 2 minutes per side. Cool to room temperature. With a pizza cutter, cut each in quarters, then cut each quarter into thirds, making 12 triangles from each quesadilla. Place on a cookie sheet and bake for 3 to 5 minutes. Can be frozen before baking. Makes 60 triangles.

GUACAMOLE DIP

1 large avocado, peeled, pitted and mashed
Salt, to taste
1 T. lemon juice
1 C. sour cream
1 pkg. taco seasoning mix

1/4 C. Monterey Jack cheese, grated
3 T. onion, grated
1/4 C. sliced black olives
1 tomato, chopped
Hot pepper sauce, to taste

Mix the avocado with the salt and lemon juice. Mix together the sour cream and taco seasoning. Layer the avocado mixture, sour cream and remaining ingredients in the order given. Serve with tortilla chips. Serves 10 to 12.

SALSA POTATO SKINS

5 large russet potatoes
1/3 C. butter, melted
3/4 C. Cheddar cheese

3/4 C. Monterey Jack cheese
Chile Salsa

Chile Salsa:
1-8 oz. can tomato sauce
1-4 oz. can diced green chilies

1/4 C. chopped green onions

Mix all the salsa ingredients, cover and refrigerate for up to a day. Bake potatoes until done. Cool. Cut each potato lengthwise into quarters. With a spoon, scoop flesh from the skins, leaving a 1/8-inch shell. Brush potato skins inside and out with the butter. Place, cut side up, in a single layer on a baking sheet. Bake in a 500 degrees F. oven for 12 minutes. Remove from the oven and distribute cheeses among the skins. Broil 4 inches from heat until cheeses are melted. Serve with sauce for dipping. Makes 20 appetizers.

BLACK BEAN CAKES

2-15 oz. cans black beans, drained
 and mashed
3 oz. shredded Monterey Jack
 cheese
8 green onions, finely chopped
1/2 C. finely chopped red bell
 pepper
1/3 C. chopped fresh cilantro
2 T. minced seeded jalapeño
3 large garlic cloves, minced

2 t. cumin
1 t. salt
1/2 t. freshly-ground pepper
2 T. yellow cornmeal
1 egg, slightly beaten
1 C. yellow cornmeal
1/4 C. vegetable oil
Sour cream
Salsa
Guacamole

Stir the first 10 ingredients together. Add 2 tablespoons cornmeal and eggs and mix well. Chill, covered, for 1 hour. Place 1 cup cornmeal in a small bowl. Drop 1 heaping tablespoon of the bean mixture into the cornmeal and roll to coat. Flatten into a 1/2-inch cake. Repeat with the rest of the mixture. Heat oil in a large heavy skillet over medium heat. Fry the cakes for 5 to 6 minutes per side. Drain on paper towels. Serve warm with the sour cream, salsa and guacamole. Makes 20 to 25.

CHEESE BALLED OLIVES

4 oz. Cheddar cheese, grated
1 t. milk
1-8 oz. pkg. cream cheese, softened
1 T. Worcestershire sauce
1/2 t. garlic powder

1 T. dried onions
1 T. dried chives
Pinch dried dill weed
1 can green or black olives,
 drained and almost dry

In a mixing bowl, blend the milk, cream cheese and Worcestershire sauce until thoroughly combined. Add the rest of the ingredients, except the olives. Add the cheese and blend. Refrigerate until the cheese looks like it has melted in with the cream. Surround each olive with about 1 1/2 teaspoonful of the cheese mixture. Stick each with a toothpick.

HOT OLIVE CHEESE PUFFS

1 C. sharp Cheddar cheese, grated
3 T. butter, softened
1/2 C. flour
1/4 t. salt
1/2 t. paprika
24 pimento-stuffed olives

Preheat oven to 400 degrees F. Blend the cheese with the butter. Stir in the flour, salt and paprika. Mix well. Wrap 1 teaspoon of dough around each olive, covering completely. Bake for 12 to 15 minutes, or until lightly browned.

FRIED JALAPEÑOS

1 jar pickled jalapeño peppers
1 C. flour
1 C. milk
2 C. oil
1 C. corn meal
2 t. season salt
1 lb. Monterey Jack cheese, grated

Slit jalapeños and remove seeds. Leave stems on. Dry peppers. Combine corn meal, flour and salt. Stuff peppers with cheese and push ends together to close. Dip peppers in milk, then roll in the corn meal/flour mixture until it sticks to the pepper. Set aside on wax paper. Heat 2 cups oil in 2-quart pan until it is very hot. Drop pepper in oil and turn frequently until light golden brown. Remove from oil and drain on paper towel.

Five days a week my body is a temple,
the other two it's an amusement park.

FRIED JALAPEÑOS II

Canned jalapeños, whole
Sharp Cheddar cheese
2 eggs, beaten

1/2 C. milk
Flour

Wash the jalapeños and remove seeds. Grate enough cheese to stuff the peppers. Dip in a mixture of the eggs and milk. Roll in the flour. Heat a deep skillet with oil until hot. Turn down the heat to medium and drop the jalapeños in. Will be done, when brown on all sides.

GRUYERE CHEESE-STUFFED CELERY

8 oz. Gruyere cheese, shredded
  and divided
1/2 C. firmly-packed fresh basil
  leaves
3 T. pine nuts

2 T. white wine vinegar
1/4 to 1/3 C. Olive oil
1 bunch celery, cut into 3-inch
  pieces

In a food processor, add 1/2 cup cheese and the next 3 ingredients. Process until smooth. With processor running, slowly pour the olive oil through food chute, blending just until mixture is smooth. Place mixture in a bowl and stir in the remaining cheese. Spoon into a heavy-duty, zip-top plastic bag. Cut a small hole in one corner of the bag and pipe mixture into the celery pieces. Makes about 3 dozen.

Friends are relatives you make for yourself.

TEX-MEX DEVILED EGGS

6 hard-cooked eggs
1 T. diced green onions
1 jalapeño pepper, seeded and
  finely chopped
1/4 C. mayonnaise

1 t. mustard
1/2 t. salt
1/4 C. shredded Cheddar cheese
Chili powder

Cut cooked eggs in half crosswise. Remove the yolks and place in a bowl. Mash. Stir in the rest of the ingredients, except the chili powder and cheese. Spoon into egg whites. Sprinkle with the cheese and chili powder. Cover and chill.

DEVILED EGGS

4 hard-boiled eggs, peeled and
  halved the long way
Salt, to taste

2 T. mayonnaise
1 t. Dijon mustard
1/4 t. cayenne

Remove the yolks and mash. Add the rest of the ingredients and mix. Add mixture back to the egg white halves. Chill.

For every drink, there is a reason!

SPINACH BALLS

1-20 oz. pkg. frozen spinach, chopped
2 C. herb stuffing mix
3/4 C. Parmesan cheese, grated

1 t. garlic, finely minced
1 medium onion, finely chopped
3 eggs, beaten
1/4 lb. butter

Preheat oven to 350 degrees F. Thaw spinach and remove excess liquid. Add remaining ingredients and mix well. Form into small balls and place on a baking sheet. Bake for 15 minutes. Dip in hot mustard.

SPINACH SPIRALS

3 pkg. cream cheese, softened
1 pkg. frozen chopped spinach, thawed and drained
2-4 oz. cans chopped green chilies

1/4 C. chopped green onions
1-6 oz. pkg. chopped ham
Salt, pepper, garlic salt, to taste
1-20 count pkg. tortillas

Blend all ingredients, except tortillas, and mix well. Spread evenly on the tortillas and roll up. Chill until set. Slice each tortilla into 1-inch pinwheels.

Few women admit their age, fewer men act theirs!

SPINACH BURRITOS

2 pkg. chopped spinach
1 C. mayonnaise
1-16 oz. ctn. sour cream
1 jar of real bacon bits

1 pkg. Hidden Valley party dip
 mix
40 flour tortillas

Thaw spinach and squeeze all water from spinach. Place in large mixing bowl. Add the remaining ingredients and mix well. Spread about 1 tablespoon of mixture on each burrito and roll up seam down. Place in a covered dish and chill for 1 hour. Then cut burrito in 3 sections and serve.

STUFFED CREAM CHEESE MUSHROOMS

2 lb. medium mushrooms
6 T. butter
1-8 oz. pkg. cream cheese, softened

1/2 C. crumbled blue cheese
2 T. chopped green onion

Remove the stems from the mushrooms. Chop the stems to equal 1/2 cup. Cook 1 pound of the mushroom caps in 3 tablespoons of the butter over medium heat for 5 minutes. Drain off fat. Repeat with the other pound. Combine the cream cheese and blue cheese, mixing well. Stir in the chopped stems and green onions. Fill in the mushroom caps. Place on a baking sheet and broil until the tops are golden brown. Makes 40.

Friends help you move. Real friends help you move the bodies!

MUSHROOM PUFFS

2 pkg. crescent dinner rolls
1-8 oz. pkg. cream cheese, room
  temperature
1-4 oz. can mushrooms, drained
  and chopped

2 green onions, chopped
1 t. seasoned salt
1 large egg, beaten
2 T. poppy seeds

Preheat oven to 375 degrees F. Lay out crescent roll dough and press perforations to seal. Mix the next 4 ingredients and spread over the dough. Roll up jellyroll style and slice into 1-inch pieces. Brush with egg and sprinkle with the poppy seeds. Bake for 10 minutes. Serve hot. Makes 48.

MARINATED MUSHROOMS

2/3 C. tarragon vinegar
1/2 C. salad oil
2 cloves garlic, halved
1 T. sugar
1 1/2 t. salt

Fresh ground pepper
2 T. water
Dash Tabasco sauce
1 onion, slice in rings
2 pt. fresh mushrooms

Combine first 8 ingredients, putting garlic on toothpicks. Add the onions and mushrooms. Cover and refrigerate for 8 hours, stirring several times.

Girls just want to have funds.

MARINATED MUSHROOMS AND CHEESE

1/2 lb. mushrooms, trimmed and
  cut into chunks
Juice of 1 lemon
1 T. extra-virgin olive oil

Salt and pepper, to taste
1/2 lb. Parmesan cheese, in 1
  chunk

Mix the lemon juice, olive oil and salt and pepper and toss with the mushrooms. Break the cheese into small chunks. Use a toothpick to skewer a mushroom and a piece of cheese. Do this with each mushroom.

SPINACH MUSHROOMS

16-20 small mushrooms, cleaned
  and trimmed
1 C. finely-chopped onion
3 T. butter

1-10 oz. pkg. frozen chopped
  spinach, cooked, drained and
  squeezed
1/2 C. grated Swiss cheese
Grated Parmesan cheese

Preheat the oven to 300 degrees F. Butter a shallow baking pan large enough to hold all the mushroom caps in 1 layer. Remove the stems. Chop the stems fine and sauté with onion in butter about 5 minutes. Add the spinach and stir to mix thoroughly. Add the Swiss cheese, stirring lightly. Remove from the heat. Fill the mushroom caps with the mixture. Sprinkle with the Parmesan cheese and place in the pan. Bake for 15 to 20 minutes.

Good girls go to heaven, bad girls go everywhere.

MUSHROOM PÂTÉ

1 lb. mushrooms, chopped
2 T. butter, melted
1-8 oz. pkg. cream cheese, softened

1/2 tsp. garlic salt
1 tsp. seasoned pepper

Sauté mushrooms in butter in a skillet over medium-high heat until liquid is absorbed. Let mushrooms cool to room temperature. In a food processor, add the mushrooms and rest of the ingredients. Process until smooth. Spoon into a greased 7 1/2x3x2-inch loaf pan. Chill. Unmold pâté. Serve with crackers. Makes 2 cups.

Guest towels are to be used by guests.
Non-guests are to use their clothing.

MUSHROOMS STUFFED WITH PESTO AND CHEESE

Olive oil
12 large firm white mushrooms,
  stems removed and caps wiped
  clean

1 small lemon, halved
1/2 C. fresh basil pesto
1/3 C. Parmesan cheese

Preheat oven to 375 degrees F. Brush bottom of baking dish with olive oil. Rub mushroom caps with lemon to prevent darkening. Brush caps with olive oil. Arrange rounded side down in single compact layer in a baking dish. Fill mushrooms with the pesto. Sprinkle tops with about 2 1/2 tablespoons of cheese. Drizzle small amount of olive oil over each.

Fresh Basil Pesto:
2 C. packed fresh basil leaves
2 large garlic cloves
1/2 C. pine nuts

3/4 C. Parmesan cheese
2/3 C. olive oil

Mince basil leaves finely. Using a mortar, crush to a fine paste. Add garlic and work into paste. Gradually add the pine nuts and crush until smooth, blend in cheese. Add olive oil to mixture in a slow steady stream, stirring constantly. You can use a food processor, also. Place the pesto in a jar and cover the top with a film of olive oil, about 1/8-inch thick. Seal jar. Refrigerate up to 3 months. Stir the oil into pesto before using.

Go braless, it pulls the wrinkles out of your face!

CAJUN STUFFED MUSHROOMS

1/2 lb. Andouille sausage
1 C. chopped onion
1/4 C. chopped bell pepper
1/2 t. salt
1/2 t. garlic powder
1/2 t. cayenne pepper
1 C. water

3/4 C. instant rice
1/4 C. parsley, chopped
24 large mushroom caps, save stems
2 C. mayonnaise
1 1/2 C. Parmesan cheese

Preheat oven to 350 degrees F. Brown the sausage, onion, bell peppers and mushroom stems. Add the salt, garlic powder and cayenne pepper. Add water and bring to a boil. Add rice and parsley. Cover and remove from heat. Let stand for 15 minutes. Blend the mayonnaise and cheese. Combine half of the mayonnaise mixture to the meat-rice mixture. Stuff mushrooms with this and spoon remaining mayonnaise mixture on top of the mushrooms. Place in a 9x12-inch dish for 35 minutes.

GRILLED MARINATED MUSHROOMS

2 lbs. fresh mushrooms
2/3 C. red wine vinegar
1/3 C. olive oil

Salt and pepper, to taste
1 clove garlic, crushed
Grated Parmesan cheese

Remove the stems from the fresh mushrooms and wipe with a clean dry cloth. Cut the stems into thick slices and place the slices and caps in 1 zipper-type plastic bag. Blend the rest of the ingredients, except the cheese. Pour over the bagged mushrooms and remove any air from the bag before sealing. Refrigerate for at least 15 minutes, but no longer than 2 hours prior to grilling. Prepare the grill. Drain the mushrooms and place in tinfoil packets. Seal tinfoil and place on the grill. Turn mushroom packets every 2 to 4 minutes, making sure to rotate them over the grill. When done, about 12 to 16 minutes, sprinkle with cheese. Reseal and cook 2 to 3 minutes longer.

CHERRY BOMBS

1 1/4 C. ricotta cheese
1/3 C. pickled jalapeño pepper
  slices

Kosher salt
Ground white pepper
48 small cherry tomatoes

Place the ricotta in a bowl. Drain jalapeños and dice to make 5 tablespoons. Add to the ricotta. Add the salt and pepper. Wash tomatoes removing any stems. Dry well. Turn tomatoes so stem end faces down. Cut a small slice from the top, which is really the bottom, and save. Scoop out insides and discard. Add the ricotta mixture to the hole so that it is rounded on top. Replace the tomato slice. Chill. Makes 48.

ASPARAGUS ROLLERS

24 slices sandwich bread, crust
  removed
1/2 C. butter, softened
1-8 oz. pkg. cream cheese, softened

4 oz. blue cheese, softened
24 fresh asparagus spears,
  partially cooked
1/2 C. butter, melted

Preheat oven to 400 degrees F. Flatten each slice of bread with a rolling pin. Mix butter with cheeses and spread on bread. Top each slice with an asparagus spear. Roll the bread around the asparagus, securing with a toothpick. Dip in melted butter and cut each roll into fourths. Freeze pieces on a cookie sheet. When ready to bake, bake for 15 minutes. Makes 8 dozen.

"Housework won't kill you, but why take a chance." Phyliss Diller

ASPARAGUS WRAPS

6 oz. blue cheese, crumbled
1-8 oz. pkg. cream cheese, softened
1 egg

1 lb. loaf white bread, crust
 removed
1-10 oz. pkg. frozen asparagus
1/2 C. butter, melted

Mix the blue cheese, cream cheese and egg. Flatten each piece of bread with a rolling pin. Spread the mixture on each piece and add 1 piece of the asparagus on each. Roll the slices. Place in freezer and freeze at least 4 hours. When ready to serve, place on a baking sheet and brush with the butter. Bake in a preheated 350 degrees F. oven and bake for 10 minutes. Cut into bite-size pieces. Makes 10 servings.

ZUCCHINI STICKS

3 C. zucchini, thinly sliced
1 C. Bisquick
1/2 C. onion, finely chopped
1/2 C. Parmesan cheese, grated
1 clove garlic, finely chopped

2 T. parsley, snipped
1/2 t. salt
1/2 t. marjoram
1/2 C. vegetable oil
4 eggs, slightly beaten

Preheat oven to 350 degrees F. Grease a 9x13x2-inch pan. Mix all the ingredients. Spread mixture in the pan. Bake for 25 minutes. Cut into pieces to make 4 dozen.

If a man speaks in the forest with no woman to hear him, is he still wrong?

ZUCCHINI FRENCH FRIES

2 eggs
1 T. water
1/4 C. + 2 T. flour

2 medium zucchini, cut into one
   inch slices
Peanut oil
Salt

Mix the eggs and water. Add the flour and beat until smooth. Dip zucchini in the batter and deep fry in hot oil until golden brown. Drain on paper towels and sprinkle with salt. Makes about 2 1/2 dozen.

BAKED GARLIC

1 large head elephant garlic
1/4 C. white wine
1/4 C. chicken stock

1 T. unsalted butter, melted
Salt
Cayenne pepper

Preheat oven to 300 degrees F. Snip off top of garlic. Place the intact head in a small ovenproof serving dish. Add the white wine and chicken stock to almost cover the garlic. Pour melted butter over the garlic. Sprinkle with salt and cayenne pepper. Bake 3 hours. To serve, pull individual cloves off head and squeeze insides onto a plate. Spread the baked garlic as you would spread soft butter on your bread.

"If life were fair, men would have stretch marks." Judge Judy

CHIPOTLE FRIED ONION RINGS

2 firm white onions, sliced thinly
and separated into rings
1/2 C. flour

1/4 t. salt
1/4 T. cumin seeds, ground
1 t. chipotle powder

Preheat the oven to 250 degrees F. and line a baking sheet with paper towels. Heat vegetable oil in a deep skillet or deep fryer to very hot and reduce heat. Mix flour, salt, cumin seeds and chipotle powder. Cover the onion rings with mixture and place in the hot oil. Cook until golden brown. Keep warm in oven.

ARKANSAS CAVIAR

2 cans white niblet corn, drained
2 cans peas, drained
2 tomatoes, finely diced
1 bell pepper, diced
1/2 C. fresh parsley, chopped
1/2 C. celery, chopped

1 T. garlic, minced
10 green onions, chopped
1/4 C. jalapeño peppers, chopped
1 large bottle Italian salad
dressing

Mix all ingredients and blend well. Refrigerate for 4 hours or overnight.

If the broom fits, ride it.

MARINATED BROCCOLI

3 bunches fresh broccoli
1 C. cider vinegar
1 1/2 C. vegetable oil
1 T. sugar
1 T. sugar

1 T. dill weed
2 t. monosodium glutamate
1 t. pepper
1 t. garlic salt

Cut the flowerets from the broccoli. Mix the remaining ingredients and pour over the flowerets. Cover and refrigerate 24 hours. Drain before serving. Serves 18.

We like wine, not whiners.

Meat
&
Poultry
Appetizers

BAKED EGG ROLLS

1 T. vegetable oil
1/2 lb. ground turkey breast
1 C. shredded cabbage
1 medium shredded carrot
2 T. green onion, finely chopped

1 T. chili paste or purée
1 T. dry white wine
1 t. cornstarch
16 frozen phyllo dough pieces,
  13x9-inches, thawed

Preheat oven to 375 degrees F. Add the oil to a skillet and heat over medium heat. Add the turkey and cook until partially browned, 5 minutes. Add the next 3 ingredients and cook until turkey is done. Stir in the chili paste. Mix the wine and cornstarch together and add to the skillet. Cook, uncovered, stirring occasionally, for 5 more minutes. Remove from the heat. Cut the dough in half crosswise and keep covered with a damp towel. Brush each with vegetable oil and top with a second piece of the dough. Place about 2 tablespoons of turkey mix on the short end of the dough. Roll dough over turkey and fold both ends over turkey and continue to roll dough around filling. Place each egg roll seam side down on a greased baking sheet and bake for 15 to 20 minutes. Makes 32.

If you can put a man on the moon, why not all of them?

USA EGG ROLLS

1 lb. ground beef
1 small head cabbage, shredded
4 large carrots, shredded
2 stalks celery, shredded
1-8 oz. jar mushrooms, chopped in small pieces
1 can bamboo shoots, chopped in small pieces

Salt and pepper, to taste
Soy sauce, to taste
2 pkg. egg roll wraps
2 eggs
4 T. water
4 T. cornstarch

Brown beef and drain off grease. Add the next 7 ingredients to the brown beef. Set aside. In a bowl, add the eggs, water and cornstarch. Place the egg wrapper in a diamond position. Cover with a film of egg mixture. Place 2 heaping tablespoons on the lower half of the wrapper and fold as if an envelope. Seal well. Deep fry. Makes 30.

MEXICAN EGG ROLLS

1 lb. ground beef
1/2 C. chopped onion
1/4 C. chopped bell pepper
1-15 oz. can refried beans
1/2 C. shredded Cheddar cheese

1 T. chili powder
2 pkg. egg roll wraps
Shortening
Taco sauce

Brown the ground beef with the onions and bell pepper. Drain off the fat. Add the beans, chili powder and cheese. Mix well until cheese is melted. Place a teaspoonful into an egg roll wrapper and fold into squares. Seal wrappers with water. Deep fry in the shortening until golden brown. Serve with the taco sauce.

RANCH MEATBALLS

1 pkg. Hidden Valley Original
   Ranch dressing mix
1 lb. ground meat

2 T. butter
1/2 C. beef broth

Combine the dressing and ground meat. Shape into meatballs. Melt the butter in a skillet and brown the meatballs on all sides. Add broth, cover and simmer until cooked through, about 10 to 15 minutes. Serve warm with toothpicks. Makes 2 dozen.

QUESADILLA MEATBALLS

1-8 oz. jar spicy black bean dip
12-8-inch flour tortillas
30 frozen cooked meatballs,
   thawed and crumbled

1-6 oz. shredded Monterey Jack
   cheese with peppers
1 green bell pepper, diced
Sour cream
Salsa

Spread the bean dip over 6 of the tortillas. Layer the crumbled meatballs, cheese and bell peppers evenly over the bean dip, top with the remaining tortillas. Cook the quesadillas in a skillet for 2 minutes on each side. Cut into 4 triangles and serve with the sour cream and salsa.

I have a furniture problem, my chest has fallen into my drawers.

SOUTH OF THE BORDER MEATBALLS

1 1/2 lbs. ground pork
1 pkg. Lawry's Taco Spices and
  seasonings
1/4 C. unseasoned dry bread
  crumbs

1 egg, beaten
1/2 C. grated onion
1/4 C. minced green pepper
1 1/2 C. chunky salsa

Mix all the ingredients, except the salsa. Form into 1-inch balls. Brown balls in a skillet with oil and drain. Add the salsa and bring to a boil. Reduce heat and simmer for 10 minutes. Serve with toothpicks.

CRANBERRY MEATBALLS

4 eggs, beaten
1 C. crushed corn flake cereal
1/3 C. chili sauce
1 T. soy sauce
1 t. dried parsley
1 T. dried onion flakes
8 hamburger patties

2 sleeves buttery round crackers,
  crumbled
1-8 oz. pkg. cream cheese, softened
1 C. chopped walnut
1-16 oz. can cranberry sauce
1 C. Russian-style salad dressing
1 t. brown sugar
1 T. lemon juice

Preheat oven to 350 degrees F. Spray two cookie sheets with Pam. In a bowl, the first 10 ingredients. Shape into 72-1-inch meatballs. Place on the cookie sheets and bake for 20 to 25 minutes. In a saucepan, combine the rest of the ingredients and cook until cranberry sauce is melted, stirring frequently. Add the meatballs and heat. Serve with toothpicks.

ORIENTAL MEATBALLS

3 lbs. ground chuck
3/4 C. soy sauce
3/4 C. water

1 clove mashed garlic
2 t. ground ginger

Preheat oven to 275 degrees F. Mix well and make into meatballs. Place on a cookie sheet. Bake for 15 minutes, turning over once.

SWEDISH MEATBALLS

2 C. bread cubes
1/2 C. milk
1 1/2 lb. ground beef
1 onion, finely chopped
2 T. margarine
2 1/2 t. salt

1 t. dry mustard
1 t. dried mixed herbs
2 t. nutmeg
1/4 t. pepper
2 t. paprika
3 eggs, beaten

Sauce:
1/4 C. margarine
1/4 t. crushed garlic
4 T. flour
2 t. tomato paste

1 t. beef concentrate
1 can beef bouillon
1 C. sour cream
1 T. Angostura bitters

Soak the bread cubes in milk. Squeeze dry. Add to the ground beef. Add the onion. Add all other ingredients, except the sauce ingredients. Mix well and form into small balls. Brown in skillet in 1/4 cup margarine. Remove the meat. Add the sauce ingredients, except the sour cream and bitters, to the skillet and make cook until sauce is made. Add the sour cream and bitters just before serving.

SWEET AND SOUR MEATBALLS

3/4 lb. extra-lean ground beef
3/4 lb. ground turkey
1 small onion, minced
1/4 C. egg substitute
1/2 C. Italian seasoned bread
  crumbs

3/4 C. ketchup
1/3 C. white vinegar
1/4 C. Worcestershire sauce
3 T. sugar
2 t. dry mustard

Mix the first 5 ingredients and shape into 1-inch balls. Brown meat balls in a nonstick skillet over medium-high heat. Remove the meatballs and wipe the skillet clean. Add the next 5 ingredients and bring to a boil. Add the meatballs, reduce heat and simmer 5 minutes. Serve with toothpicks. Makes 3 1/2 dozen.

PORK MEATBALLS

1 lb. ground pork
1/2 C. soft bread crumbs
1 egg, beaten
2 T. minced onion
1 T. minced green pepper
1 clove garlic, minced

1 t. salt
1/8 t. pepper
1 T. vegetable oil
1-8 oz. can tomato sauce
1/4 C. apple jelly
1/4 t. curry powder

Combine the first 8 ingredients. Mix well. Shape into 30-1-inch balls. Brown the balls in the oil in a skillet and drain well. In a saucepan, add the rest of the ingredients and warm until the jelly is melted, stirring occasionally. Pour over the meatballs, cover and simmer for 15 to 20 minutes, stirring often.

TAMALE BALLS

2-16 oz. cans tomatoes, undrained
    and puréed
1 1/2 t. chili powder
1/2 t. salt
1/2 lb. ground pork
1/2 lb. ground beef

3/4 C. cornmeal
2 T. flour
1/3 C. tomato juice
2 small cloves garlic, crushed
1 1/2 t. chili powder
1 t. salt

Combine first 3 ingredients in a saucepan. Bring mixture to a boil over medium heat. In a bowl, add the remaining ingredients. Mix well. Shape into 1-inch balls and add to the sauce. Simmer meatballs 1 hour. Makes 4 dozen meatballs.

SAUSAGE BALLS

1 lb. ground spicy chicken or
    turkey sausage
1 egg, slightly beaten
1/3 c. unseasoned fine bread
    crumbs
1/2 t. dried sage

1/4 C. chili sauce
1/4 C. catsup
1 t. brown sugar
1 t. soy sauce
1 T. white vinegar

Mix the sausage, egg, bread crumbs and sage. Shape into 4 dozen balls. Brown the balls in a skillet with a little oil. Drain the fat. Combine the rest of the ingredients in the skillet and simmer the balls for 10 to 15 minutes. Serve warm with toothpicks.

MARINATED SIRLOIN

1-10 to 12 lb. beef sirloin
16 oz. Italian salad dressing
1/2 C. white vinegar
8 oz. jalapeño pepper, drained and
  sliced

1 T. oregano
1 T. Cavender's Greek seasoning
1 T. Italian seasoning
16 oz. sour cream

Broil sirloin to rare. Thinly slice the sirloin and julienne the slices. Add all the ingredients, except the sour cream, and mix. Pour over the sirloin and marinate overnight. Drain slices well in a colander. Remove the jalapeño slices. Toss the meat with the sour cream. Serve with pumpernickel or melba rye rounds. Serves 35 to 50.

SUPER NACHOS

2-16 oz. cans refried beans
1 1/2 lb. ground meat
1 onion, chopped
1-4 oz. can chopped green chilies
3 C. Cheddar cheese, grated
2-4 oz. cans taco sauce

Chopped green onions
Sliced ripe olives
Sour cream
Guacamole
Chips

Preheat oven to 400 degrees F. Spread refried beans in a large oblong pan. Brown the meat and onions. Drain, layer over the beans. Sprinkle the green chilies over the meat. Cover with the cheese and taco sauce. Bake for 25 to 30 minutes. Remove from oven and spread with chopped green onions and olives. Before serving, garnish with the sour cream and guacamole.

HANKY PANKS

1 to 2 loaves cocktail bread
2 lbs. ground meat
1 lb. Velveeta cheese, cubed

1/2 T. garlic salt
1/2 T. oregano
1/2 T. Worcestershire sauce

Preheat oven to 375 degrees F. Brown meat. Drain the meat. Add the cheese and spices. Simmer until cheese melts. Spread on cocktail bread and freeze. Take out of freezer and bake for 10 to 15 minutes.

BITE-SIZE TACO TURNOVERS

1/2 lb. ground beef
1/4 C. taco sauce
2 t. chili powder
1/4 t. onion powder
1/4 t. garlic powder

1-10 oz. pkg. refrigerated pizza
    dough
1/4 C. shredded American cheese
1 egg
1 t. water

Preheat oven to 425 degrees F. Brown the ground beef in a skillet. Drain off fat. Stir in the taco sauce, chili powder, onion powder and garlic powder. Set aside. Unroll pizza dough. Roll the dough into a 14x10 1/2-inch rectangle. Cut into twelve 3 1/2-inch squares. Divide filling between the 12 squares. Sprinkle with cheese. Brush edges with water. Lift one corner of each square and stretch dough to the opposite corner, making a triangle. Press edges well with a fork to seal. Place on a greased baking sheet. Prick with fork. Combine the egg and water. Brush onto the turnovers. Bake for 8 to 10 minutes. Makes 12.

HOT WINGS

1-5 lb. frozen wings
1/2 lb. butter, melted

1-32 oz. bottle hot sauce

Preheat oven to 375 degrees F. In a large pan, add all the ingredients. Bake for 1 1/2 hours.

BAKED CHICKEN WINGS

5 lbs. chicken wings
1 C. soy sauce
3 t. salt
2 t. pepper
3 t. paprika

3 T. lemon juice
3 T. sugar
1 C. water
3 T. oleo, melted
1 T. garlic powder

Preheat oven to 350 degrees F. Mix all the ingredients, except the chicken wings. Pour over the wings and marinate for 4 to 24 hours. Bake, uncovered, for 25 minutes and broil for 5 to 15 minutes.

It's hard to be optimistic when your "fat" pants are tight.

BARBEQUED CHICKEN WINGS

12 chicken wings, about 2 lbs.
1/4 C. catsup
2 T. water
2 T. finely-chopped onion
1 T. cooking oil
1 1/2 t. vinegar
1 t. brown sugar

1 t. Worcestershire sauce
1/4 t. dried oregano, crushed
1/4 t. chili powder
1/4 t. dry mustard
1 bay leaf
1 clove garlic, minced

Cut off and discard tips of chicken wings. Cut wings at joints to form 24 pieces. Place the 24 chicken wing pieces in a single layer in an ungreased 13x9x2-inch baking pan. Bake in a 375 degree F. oven for 20 minutes. Drain well. Meanwhile, for barbecue sauce, in a saucepan combine catsup, water, onion, cooking oil, vinegar, brown sugar, Worcestershire sauce, oregano, chili powder, mustard, bay leaf and garlic. Bring mixture to boiling, then reduce heat. Simmer, covered, for 10 minutes, stirring occasionally. Discard bay leaf. Brush barbecue sauce on the partially baked chicken wings. Bake for 10 minutes, then turn and brush barbecue sauce on the other side. Bake for 5 to 10 minutes more, or until chicken is tender. Makes 12.

Who invited all these tacky people?

TEX-MEX CHICKEN MUNCHIES

2 C. chicken, cooked and shredded
1 t. chili powder
Tabasco sauce, to taste
1-4 oz. can chopped green chilies
1-4 oz. can black olives, chopped
  and drained

1/4 C. green onion tops, finely
  chopped
1/2 C. Monterey Jack cheese,
  grated
1 lb. pkg. wonton wrappers
Salsa

In a bowl, add the first 7 ingredients and mix well. Place 1 teaspoon of chicken mixture in the center of each wonton wrapper. Fold one corner over filling. Fold in sides with points overlapping. Wet edges slightly to seal. Fold the final corner down sealing edge. Drop in preheated oil and fry until brown and crisp. Remove and serve on a paper towel to drain. Serve with the salsa. Makes 12 servings.

BOURBON CHICKEN

1 lb. chicken thigh meat cut into
  large bite size chunks
1/2 C. soy sauce
1/2 C. brown sugar
1/2 t. garlic powder

1 t. powdered ginger
2 T. dried minced onion
1/2 C. Jim Beam Bourbon whiskey
2 T. white wine

Mix all the ingredients, except the chicken meat and wine, and pour over the chicken pieces in a bowl. Cover and refrigerate stirring often for at least 2 hours or overnight. Preheat oven to 350 degrees F. Bake for 1 hour, basting every 10 minutes. Remove the chicken from the pan. Scrape the pan juices into a frying pan. Heat and add the wine. Stir and add the chicken and cook for 1 minute more. Serve with toothpicks.

RUMAKI

16 chicken liver   1/2 C. sherry
1 C. soy sauce   16 slices bacon, halved crosswise

Wash chicken livers and dry with paper towels. Cut each in half. Place in a large bowl. Mix the soy sauce and sherry and pour over the livers and toss lightly. Wrap each liver with a slice of bacon. Secure with a wooden toothpick. Place on a broiler pan. Brush both sides with the soy mixture. Broil 3-inches from the heat, turning once or twice at 2- to 4- minute intervals. Cook until bacon is done. Makes 32.

EASY AS 1-2-3

1 lb. bulk pork sausage   3-5 oz. jars Old English brand
2 C. flour   process cheese

Preheat oven to 325 degrees F. Mix all ingredients. Shape into small balls, flatten into round cookie shapes and place on an ungreased cookie sheet. Bake for 20 minutes. Makes about 60.

I hope my ship comes in before my dock rots.

ARMADILLA EGGS

1/2 lb. hot bulk sausage
1-8 oz. pkg. cream cheese, softened
1/2 C. chopped pecans

2-26 oz. cans mild jalapeño
  peppers, drained and halved

Brown sausage in a large skillet over medium-high heat, stirring until it crumbles. Drain well. Combine sausage, cream cheese and pecans in a medium bowl. Spoon mixture into pepper halves. Cover and chill until ready to serve. Makes 2 dozen.

BACON AND DATE APPETIZER

1-8 oz. pkg. pitted dates
4 oz. almonds

1 lb. slice bacon

Slit dates. Place 1 almond inside each date. Wrap dates with the bacon, using toothpicks to hold them together. Broil for 10 minutes, or until bacon is done.

If you want a thing done well, get a couple of old broads to do it.

PEPPERONI CHEESE MUNCHERS

2 C. biscuit mix
1 C. buttermilk
2 eggs
1-3.5 oz. pkg. slice pepperoni,
  chopped

1 C. Mozzarella cheese, shredded
4 oz. Feta cheese
1/4 C. butter, melted

Preheat oven to 350 degrees F. Butter a 9x13-inch baking dish. In a bowl, mix the biscuit mix, buttermilk and eggs. Fold in the pepperoni and Mozzarella cheese. Pour into pan and spread evenly. Crumble the Feta cheese over the top and drizzle with the melted butter. Bake for 30 to 35 minutes. Cool and cut into triangles.

I'm preparing dinner as fast as I can dial!

MINI-QUICHES

Pastry:
2 C. flour
1/2 t. salt
1/2 t. chili powder
1/3 C. butter

1/3 C. vegetable shortening
1 egg, beaten
1/4 C. cold water

Mix the flour and salt. Add the chili powder. With a pastry blender, cut in the butter and shortening until the mixture resembles fine crumbs. Add the egg and cold water. Add the flour mixture 1 tablespoon at a time, mixing until dough clings together. Shape into a ball. Roll out the dough 1/16-inch thick. Cut into 2-inch circle, until you have 72. Place in tiny muffin pans.

Filling:
3/4 C. finely-diced cooked ham
3 T. chopped canned green chilies
1/4 C. green onions, chopped

1 1/2 C. Monterey Jack cheese, shredded
2 eggs
3/4 C. sour cream

Preheat oven to 375 degrees F. Mix all the ingredients, except the eggs and sour cream, and place 1 heaping teaspoon in each cup. Mix the eggs and sour cream well. Spoon over the ham mixture in equal parts. Bake for 20 to 25 minutes. Cool on wire racks and serve at room temperature.

I take life with a grain of salt, a wedge of lime and a shot of tequila!

HAM ROLLS WITH MUSHROOMS

1 lb. mushrooms, cleaned and
  trimmed
1/3 C. shallots, minced
4 T. butter
2-3 oz. pkg. cream cheese, softened
2 t. Dijon mustard

Pinch of cayenne pepper
Lemon juice, to taste
Salt and pepper, to taste
1 lb. baked ham, sliced thin
1 bunch watercress, cleaned and
  chopped

Chop the mushrooms fine and dry. Cook the shallots in the butter over moderate heat, stirring until translucent. Add the mushrooms and cook until the liquid is evaporated. Remove the skillet from the heat and stir in the cream cheese, mustard, cayenne, salt, pepper and lemon juice. Pour into a bowl and let cool. Lay the ham slices flat and spread about 2 tablespoons of the mushroom mixture on each slice. Sprinkle each slice with 1 tablespoon of the chopped watercress. Roll up the ham. Chill, covered, for at least 1 hour. Cut each roll crosswise into 4 sections. Makes about 6 dozen.

HAM BALL

1 bunch green onions, thinly
  sliced
2 small pkg. Buddig sliced
  smoked ham, diced

1-8 oz. pkg. cream cheese, softened
1 T. mayonnaise
1 t. lemon juice

Mix all the ingredients. Shape into a ball and wrap in cellophane. Refrigerate for 2 hours or more. Serve with crackers. Serves 12.

RIB BITES

16 individual pork spareribs   1 1/4 C. balsamic vinegar
1 C. unsulfured molasses

Using a cleaver, cut each rib into 2 short pieces, or have your butcher do it. You will have 32 pieces about 2 3/4-inches long. Place in large shallow casserole. Combine molasses and vinegar in small bowl. Add 1 teaspoon salt and freshly-ground black pepper. Pour over ribs. Cover and refrigerate for 2 hours, turning every 30 minutes. Preheat oven to 375 degrees F. Remove ribs from marinade. Transfer marinade to small saucepan. Place ribs on 1 or 2 baking sheets. Bake for 40 minutes. Turn and bake for 35 minutes more. Meanwhile, bring marinade to a boil. Lower heat and simmer until reduced to a syrup, about 10 to 15 minutes. Add salt and pepper, if desired. Remove ribs from baking sheet, discarding all the fat. Using a pastry brush, paint each rib with reduced marinade. Place on platter and serve with lots of napkins. Makes 32 bits.

I was put on this earth to embarrass my teenagers!

CHINESE-STYLE BARBEQUED RIBS

2 1/2-3 lbs. rack fresh pork back
  ribs, cut lengthwise across bones
  into halves
1/2 C. catsup
2 T. sugar

1 T. salt
2 T. Hoisin sauce
1 T. dry white wine
2 large cloves garlic, finely
  chopped

Trim fat and remove membranes from ribs and place ribs in shallow glass dish. Mix ingredients. Pour mixture over ribs and turn ribs. Cover and refrigerate at least 2 hours. Place ribs in single layer on rack in roasting pan and brush with sauce. Bake, uncovered, in 400 degree F. oven 30 minutes. Turn ribs and brush with sauce. Reduce oven temperature to 375 degrees F. it ribs are thin. Bake, uncovered until done, about 30 minutes longer. Cut between each rib. Makes 3 dozen. Serve with Hot Mustard, if desired.

Hot Mustard:
1/2 C. dry mustard   3 T. cold water

Stir dry mustard and water together until smooth. Let stand 5 minutes before serving.

MANDARIN PORK KABOBS

1 lb. boneless pork loin, cut into 16
  thin strips
1-11 oz. can mandarin oranges,
  drained
1 small green pepper, cut into 1/2-
  inch chunks
1/4 C. reduced-sodium teriyaki
  sauce

1 T. honey
1 T. vinegar
1/8 t. garlic powder
16 bamboo skewers, soaked in
  cold water for 20 to 30 minutes
  prior to assembly

Mix the teriyaki sauce, honey, vinegar and garlic powder and mix well. Pour over the pork and marinate in the refrigerator. Thread pork strips, accordion-style on the skewers, alternating mandarin oranges and green pepper pieces and ending with another pork strip. Baste the meat, oranges and green pepper during the cooking. Broil for 5 to 6 minutes, turning frequently. Makes 8 servings.

MINI REUBENS

1/2 C. Thousand Island dressing
24 slices party rye bread
1 1/2 C. chopped sauerkraut,
  drained

1/2 lb. thinly-sliced corned beef
1/4 lb. sliced Swiss cheese

Preheat oven to 400 degrees F. Spread 1/2 teaspoon dressing on each slice of bread. Place 1 tablespoon sauerkraut on each slice of the bread and top with a slice of corned beef. Cut cheese the size of the bread and place over the corned beef. Arrange on a baking sheet and bake for 10 minutes, or until cheese melts. Makes 2 dozen.

BRAUNSCHWEIGER PATE

Judy Neemann, West Point, NE.

1-8 oz. pkg. cream cheese
1-8 oz. pkg. Braunschweiger
2 T. grated onion
1 T. Worcestershire sauce

1 T. lemon juice
Parsley and chives
Crackers

Combine all, except parsley, chives and crackers. Shape into roll or loaf.
Sprinkle with chives and parsley. Chill.

One tequila, two tequila, three tequila, floor.

Notes

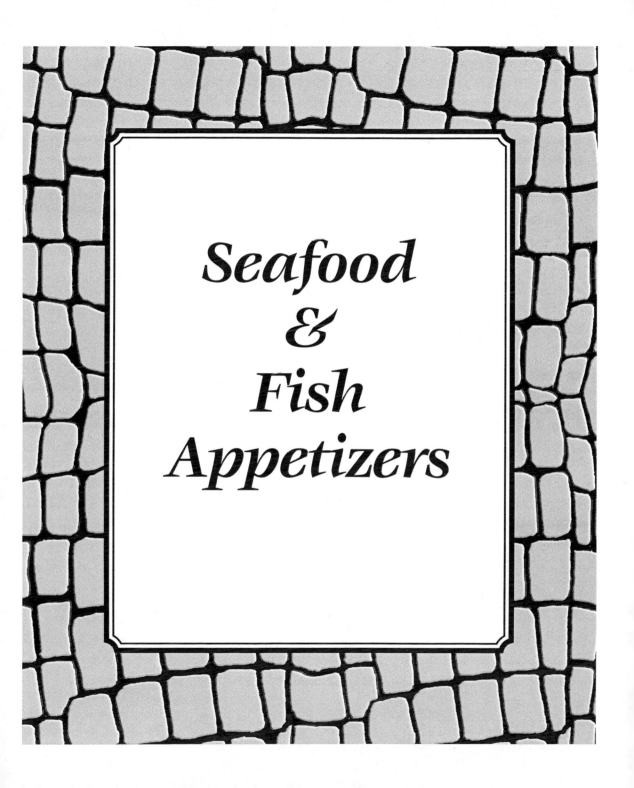

Seafood & Fish Appetizers

DOT'S CRABBIES

Virginia Truitt, Sassy Selections, Martinsville, VA.

1 stick butter or margarine
1 lb. crabmeat
1 jar Old English cheese spread
1/2 C. mayonnaise, I use
  Hellmann's

1/2 t. garlic salt
1/2 t. seasoned salt
6 English muffins

Soften the butter and cheese at room temperature. Mix the mayonnaise, garlic salt and salt. Add the crabmeat. Spread on halves of the muffins. Freeze until solid on a cookie sheet. Cut each muffin into 8 pie shaped wedges. Store in plastic bags in freezer until ready to use. Broil until bubbly. Makes 96.

CRAB AND ARTICHOKE TARTS

1-4 oz. carton egg substitute
2 t. flour
1/8 t. dried thyme
1/4 t. salt
1/8 t. black pepper
1/3 C. bottled roasted red bell
  peppers, drained and chopped

1-14 oz. can artichoke hearts,
  drained and chopped
1-6 oz. can crabmeat, drained and
  flaked
32 won ton wrappers
3 T. Parmesan cheese, grated
2 T. chopped green onions
1 T. butter, melted

Preheat oven to 350 degrees F. Mix the first 5 ingredients. Add the next 3 ingredients. Stir well. Spray 32 miniature muffin cups with Pam. Press 1 won ton wrapper into each muffin cup, allowing ends to extend above edges of cups. Spoon the crab mixture into each cup and sprinkle with the cheese and green onions. Brush edges with butter. Bake for 20 minutes. Use a toothpick to remove each one. Makes 32.

CRAB PUFF

1 C. water
1/2 C. butter
1 C. flour
4 eggs

2 C. cooked crab
1/4 C. celery, minced
3 T. grated onion
3 T. mayonnaise

Preheat oven to 400 degrees F. Mix the crab, celery, onion and mayonnaise and refrigerate. Bring the water and butter to a boil over medium heat. Stir in the flour and stir over medium heat, until mixture forms a ball. Remove from the heat and beat eggs in, one at a time. Beat mixture until smooth. Drop by spoonfuls onto ungreased baking sheet. Bake for 30 to 35 minutes. Cool. Cut off tops and scoop out the center of the dough balls. Fill with crab filling, replace tops and refrigerate. Makes 20 servings.

HOT CRAB MUFFINS

1/2 C. margarine, softened
1-5 oz. Old English cheese
1 1/2 t. mayonnaise
1-6 oz. pkg. frozen crabmeat, thawed

1-6 count pkg. English muffins, halved
Garlic powder, to taste

Combine first 4 ingredients and spread over 12 halved muffins. Sprinkle with garlic powder; cut into fourths. Bake at 400 degrees for 10 to 15 minutes; then broil for about 2 minutes or until bubbly. Can be frozen. Makes 48 appetizers.

CAJUN CRABMEAT MOLD

2-8 oz. pkg. cream cheese, softened
2 T. dairy sour cream
1/2 t. salt
1/2 t. paprika
1/2 t. ground red pepper

1/4 t. garlic powder
1/4 t. ground thyme
1 C. cooked crabmeat
1/4 finely-chopped green pepper
Rye crackers

Beat all ingredients, except crabmeat, green pepper and crackers, in 2 1/2-quart bowl on medium speed until well blended, about 1 minute. Stir in crabmeat and green pepper. Line a deep 1 1/2-pint bowl with plastic wrap and press mixture in bowl. Cover and refrigerate until firm, about 3 hours. Unmold on serving platter and remove plastic wrap. Garnish with chili peppers, if desired. Serve with crackers. Makes 3 cups.

CRAB QUICHES

1-6 count refrigerated flaky dinner
  rolls
1-6 oz. can crabmeat, drained,
  flaked and cartilage removed

1/2 C. shredded Swiss cheese
1 egg
1/2 C. milk
1/2 t. dried dill weed

Separate each dinner roll into 4 layers. Place each section in a greased 1 3/4-inch-diameter muffin cup, pressing the dough onto bottom and up sides of muffin cup. Sprinkle 1 rounded teaspoon crab into each muffin cup. Sprinkle 1 teaspoon cheese over crab. In a bowl, combine egg, milk and dill weed. Spoon about 1 1/2 teaspoons egg mixture into each muffin pan. Bake in a 375 degree F. oven about 20 minutes, or until golden. Remove from pans. Serve warm. Makes 24.

CRAB ROLL-UPS WITH AVOCADO DIP

Avocado Dip:
1 avocado, cut up
2 T. mayonnaise or salad dressing
1 T. lemon juice
1/2 t. salt

1/8 t. garlic powder
1/8 t. red pepper sauce
1 tomato, finely chopped

Place all ingredients, except tomato, in blender container. Cover and blend on high speed, stopping blender occasionally to scrape sides, until smooth, about 1 minute. Spoon into small bowl; stir in tomato. Cover and refrigerate.

1-6 1/2 oz. can crabmeat, drained
  and cartilage removed
1/2 C. shredded Monterey Jack
  cheese
1 small zucchini, shredded
1/4 C. finely-chopped celery

1/4 C. finely-chopped onion
3 T. chili sauce
1/2 t. salt
10 slices white sandwich bread
3 T. margarine or butter, melted

Mix crabmeat, cheese, zucchini, celery, onion, chili sauce and salt. Remove crusts from bread. Roll each slice to about 1/4-inch thickness. Spoon crabmeat mixture across center of each slice of bread. Bring sides of bread up over crabmeat mixture; secure with wooden picks. Place roll-ups, seam sides down, in ungreased rectangular baking dish, 13x9x2-inches and brush with margarine. Bake, uncovered, in 350 degrees F. oven until golden brown, about 30 minutes. Remove picks and cut each roll-up into 3 pieces. Serve with avocado dip. Makes 30.

"It's so great to find that one special person you want to annoy for the rest of your life." Rita Rudner

PARTY CRABMEAT

2 lbs. lump crabmeat
1/2 C. finely-chopped scallions
2 t. butter
2 T. yogurt, or as needed

2 T. mayonnaise
1/4 t. salt
Pepper, to taste
2 t. lemon juice

Pick over the crabmeat to remove any bits of shell and cartilage. Lightly spray a 4 1/2 cup decorative mold with vegetable oil cooking spray. In a nonstick skillet, sauté the scallions in butter until slightly limp. Remove from the heat and allow to cool. In a small mixing bowl, stir together the 2 tablespoons of yogurt, the mayonnaise, salt, pepper and lemon juice and blend in the cooled scallions. Add more yogurt if you want a creamier sauce. Toss the crabmeat and sauce together gently until the crab is thoroughly moistened. Pack into the prepared mold, cover with plastic wrap, and refrigerate for at least 3 hours. Unmold onto a serving plate and serve with crackers. Makes 4 cups.

LAYERED CRAB DIP

1-8 oz. pkg. cream cheese, softened
1/2 C. sour cream
1/4 C. mayonnaise
2 t. Worcestershire sauce
2 t. dry onion flakes
3/4 C. chili sauce

2-4 3/4 oz. cans crabmeat, drained
    and flaked
2 C. shredded Mozzarella cheese
Paprika
Fresh parsley

Combine cream cheese, sour cream, mayonnaise, Worcestershire sauce and onion flakes in a bowl. Spread mixture over a 12-inch dish. Spread chili sauce over sour cream cheese mixture. Layer crab and cheese over chili sauce; sprinkle with paprika. Garnish with parsley. Cover and refrigerate at least 2 hours before serving. Serve with crackers. Makes 6 to 8 servings.

SHRIMP QUICHES

1-8 oz. pkg. refrigerated butter
  flake dinner rolls
3/4 C. small cooked shrimp
1/2 C. whipping cream
2 T. green onions, finely minced

1/2 t. salt
1/4 t. dill weed
1/8 t. cayenne
1/2 C. Swiss cheese, shredded

Preheat oven to 375 degrees F. Grease 2 dozen 1 3/4-inch muffin cups. Separate rolls into 12 equal pieces. Cut each in half. Press each half in the bottom and sides of a muffin cup. Divide shrimp evenly among pastry shells. Beat together egg, cream, onion, salt, dill and cayenne until well blended. Place about 2 tablespoons of mixture in each cup. Sprinkle cheese over tops. Bake, uncovered, for 20 minutes or until edges are brown and centers appear set. Cool 5 minute and serve. Makes 24.

SHRIMP NACHOS

2 C. water
1/2 lb. unpeeled medium-size
  fresh shrimp
1-4 oz. can diced green chilies,
  drained

1-2 1/4 oz. can sliced pitted ripe
  olives, drained
6 oz. shredded Cheddar cheese
1/2 C. sliced green onions
1/2 C. mayonnaise
8 dz. round tortilla chips

Preheat oven to 350 degrees F. In a saucepan, add the water and bring to a boil. Add the shrimp and cook 3 to 5 minutes. Drain well. Rinse with cold water. Peel and devein shrimp. Coarsely chop the shrimp. Add the shrimp and next 5 ingredients. Place the chips on a baking sheet and top each with 1 1/2 teaspoons of the shrimp mixture. Bake for 5 minutes, or until cheese melts. Makes 8 dozen.

TEQUILA LIME SHRIMP

2 lbs. shrimp
2 C. julienned jicama
1/2 C. vegetable oil
1/4 C. tequila
1/3 C. sugar

1/2 C. fresh cilantro, chopped
4 jalapeño chilies, seeded and
 finely chopped
2 green onions, thinly sliced

Cover the shrimp with water in a large saucepan. Bring to a boil. Boil until the shrimp turn pink. Drain. Peel and devein the shrimp. Place the shrimp and jicama in a sealable plastic bag. Whisk the oil and tequila in a bowl. Whisk in the sugar. Stir in the rest of the ingredients. Pour over the shrimp and refrigerate for 2 hours, turning occasionally. Remove the shrimp from the bag. Pour the remaining marinade on platter with sides. Serves 8.

A man's home is his castle until the queen arrives.

PICKLED SHRIMP

2 1/2 lbs. shrimp
1/2 C. celery tops
3 1/2 t. salt
1/4 C. crab boil
Sliced onion rings
7 to 8 bay leaves

1 1/4 C. salad oil
3/4 C. white vinegar
1 1/2 t. salt
2 1/2 T. capers with juice
2 1/2 t. celery seed
Dash of Tabasco sauce

Place the shrimp in boiling water to cover. Add the next 4 ingredients. Cook shrimp 10 to 12 minutes. Drain shrimp, peel and devein. Alternate shrimp and sliced onion rings in shallow dish. Add the bay leaves. Combine the oil, vinegar, salt, celery seed, capers and Tabasco sauce. Mix well and pour over the shrimp and onions. Cover and store in refrigerator for at least 24 hours.

SHRIMP PATE

Judy Neemann, West Point, NE.

1/2 C. butter
1 T. minced onion
1 T. lemon juice
1 t. Worcestershire sauce
Dash of salt

3-4 1/2 oz. cans small shrimp,
    drained
1/2 to 3/4 C. mayonnaise
Parsley and lemon slices for
    garnish
Crackers

Melt butter in pan and stir in onion, lemon juice, Worcestershire sauce and salt until heated. Mash shrimp with fork until flaky and add butter sauce. Blend in mayonnaise, 1 tablespoon at a time, until shrimp mixture is spreading consistency. Put in mold, cover and refrigerate at least 1 hour. Unmold and garnish.

SHRIMP PASTE

4 1/2 oz. canned deveined shrimp
5 T. Miracle Whip
2 t. finely-minced onion

1/4 t. salt
1/8 t. curry powder

Drain the shrimp and soak in ice water for 20 minutes. Mash the shrimp. Add the rest of the ingredients. Refrigerate for at least an hour. Serve with crackers or toast.

SHRIMP TOAST

1/2 lb. fresh or frozen raw shrimp, thawed
1/2 C. chopped green onions with tops
1/4 C. flour
1/4 C. water
1 egg

1 T. cornstarch
1 t. salt
1/4 t. sugar
1/4 t. sesame oil
Dash of white pepper
Vegetable oil
5 slices white bread

Peel shrimp. Make a shallow cut lengthwise down back of each shrimp; wash out sand vein. Cut shrimp lengthwise into halves; cut cross-wise into halves. Mix shrimp, onions, flour, water, egg, cornstarch, salt, sugar, sesame oil and pepper. Heat oil in wok to 350 degrees F. Remove crust from bread; cut each slice into 4 squares. Place 1 or 2 pieces shrimp with sauce on each bread square. Fry 5 squares at a time, turning frequently, until golden brown, about 2 minutes; drain. Cover and refrigerate no longer than 24 hours. Heat, uncovered, in 400 degree F. oven until hot, 12 to 15 minutes; drain. Makes 20.

SHRIMP TACO

1-8 oz. pkg. cream cheese, softened
1/4 C. heavy cream
1/2 bottle chili sauce
1-4 oz. can cooked tiny shrimp, drained, rinsed and patted dry
6 scallions, chopped

3/4 C. chopped green bell pepper
1-3 or 4 oz. can pitted black olives, drained, patted dry and sliced
1-8 oz. pkg. grated Mozzarella cheese

Mix the cream cheese and the heavy cream. Pat down on a platter in an even layer. Spread with the remaining ingredients in the order that they appear above. Chill at least 1 hour before serving. Serve with tortilla chips. This can be made a day ahead provided the shrimp and olives are well drained and patted dry. Serves 8.

LOBSTER CANAPES

2 1/2 dz.-2-inch bread rounds, cut from thin sliced bread
Salad oil
1-5 oz. can lobster, shredded
1/2 C. canned condensed cream of mushroom soup

2 T. cooking sherry
1 T. chopped pimento
1/4 t. salt
Hot pepper sauce
1/4 C. buttered fine dry bread crumbs

Preheat oven to 225 degrees F. Brush bread rounds lightly with oil. Place on a cookie sheet. Cook for 1 1/4 to 1 1/2 hours, or until dry and crisp. Combine remaining ingredients, except bread crumbs. Spread mixture on the bread and sprinkle with the bread crumbs. Broil 2 to 3 minutes, or until crumbs are browned. Serve hot. Makes 30.

SEAFOOD TARTS

1 loaf very thin white bread
1/2 C. butter, melted
1 C. mayonnaise
3 oz. crabmeat
3 oz. deveined peeled cooked
  shrimp

1/3 C. fresh grated Parmesan
  cheese
1/3 C. grated Swiss cheese
1/3 C. onion, chopped
1/2 t. Worcestershire sauce
3 drops Tabasco sauce
Paprika, to taste

Preheat the oven to 400 degrees F. Remove the crusts from the bread. Flatten slightly with a rolling pin. Cut rounds from the centers of each slice with a 3-inch round cutter. Dip each round into the butter. Press the rounds into miniature muffin cups. Bake for 10 minutes. Combine the rest of the ingredients, except the paprika, into a food processor. Pulse slightly or just until mixed. Spoon this mixture into the muffin cups. Sprinkle with paprika. Bake for 10 minutes. Serve immediately. Makes 25 tarts.

Ever stop to think and forget to start again?

CEVICHE

This takes several days, but is well worth it.

3/4 lb. red snapper fillets, cut in 1x1/2-inch pieces
8 oz. small shrimp, peeled and deveined

6 oz. scallops
6 limes

Place the seafood in a glass bowl and cover with the juice of the limes. Marinate overnight. Drain and return the seafood to the bowl.

Marinade:
1 C. white onion, chopped fine and divided into 2 equal parts
4 Serrano peppers, chopped
2 tomatoes, finely chopped
1/2 C. minced green olives with pimento
1/4 C. parsley, chopped fine

1 t. chopped fresh cilantro
2 T. jalapeño pepper, chopped fine
1 T. Worcestershire sauce
2 T. crushed dry oregano leaves
3/4 C. tomato juice
Salt, to taste

Mix 1/2 cup chopped onion, tomatoes, olives, parsley, Serrano peppers and cilantro. Mix. Stir in the rest of the ingredients and pour over the fish. Marinate for 1 day in the refrigerator. Serve in margarita glasses with fresh avocado slices and cilantro. It can be refrigerated for up to 5 days. Serves 6.

I'm looking for true love, but I'll settle for cheap sex!

CAVIAR PIE

12 hard-boiled eggs
Mayonnaise
Salt and pepper, to taste
2 bunches scallion, chopped

1-8 oz. pkg. cream cheese, softened
1-16 oz. ctn. sour cream
2 large jars black caviar
1 large jar red caviar

Grease a 10-inch springform pan with a little mayonnaise. Mash the eggs and mayonnaise just enough to hold eggs together. Salt and pepper. Spread into bottom of pan. Spread scallions on top of the eggs. Mix cream cheese and sour cream until smooth. Spread over the scallions. Spread the caviar on top. Refrigerate until set. Unmold. Serve with crackers.

SUSHI ROLL

1 1/3 C. water
2/3 C. uncooked short grain white
   rice
3 T. rice vinegar
3 T. sugar
1 1/2 t. salt
4 sheets nori-seaweed sheets

1/2 cucumber, peeled, cut into
   small strips
2 T. pickled ginger
1 avocado, peeled, pitted and cut
   into small strips
1/2 lb. imitation crabmeat, flake

Preheat oven to 300 degrees F. Bring the water to a boil and add the rice. Reduce heat, cover and simmer for 20 minutes. In a bowl, add the vinegar, sugar and salt. Blend the mixture into the rice. Heat the nori for 1 to 3 minutes. Center one sheet nori on a bamboo sushi mat. Wet your hands. Spread a thin layer of rice on the nori and press down. Arrange 1/4 of the cucumber, ginger, avocado and crabmeat in a line down the center of the rice. Lift the end of the mat, and gently roll it over the ingredients, pressing gently. Roll it forward to make a complete roll. Repeat with the other 3 sheets of nori. Cut each roll into 4 to 6 slices.

SMOKED SALMON SUSHI ROLL

2 C. Japanese sushi rice
6 T. rice wine vinegar
6 sheets nori-dry seaweed
1 avocado, peeled, pitted and
  sliced

1 cucumber, peeled and sliced
8 oz. smoked salmon, cut into long
  strips
2 T. wasabi paste

Soak rice for 4 hours. Drain rice and cook in a rice cooker with 2 cups of water. When rice is cooked, mix in vinegar. Spread rice on a plate until cool. Place 1 sheet of seaweed on a bamboo mat, press a thin layer of rice on the seaweed. Leave at least 1/2-inch top and bottom edge of the seaweed uncovered. Dot some wasabi on the rice. Arrange the cucumber, avocado and salmon to the rice. Do not place 1-inch from the bottom edge. Slightly wet the top edge of the seaweed. Roll from bottom to the top edge. Cut roll into 8 equal pieces and serve.

SALMON BALL

8 oz. salmon
1-8 oz. pkg. cream cheese
1 t. liquid smoke

1 t. horseradish
1 t. lemon juice
Chopped walnuts or pecans

Blend together and form into a ball. Roll in chopped nuts of your choice.

I'm not aging, I'm marinating!

SALMON BALL II

1-16 oz. can red salmon, drained
11 oz. cream cheese, softened
1 T. chopped onion
2 t. lemon juice

1 1/2 t. horseradish
1 t. Worcestershire sauce
1/4 t. liquid smoke

Mix all the ingredients and shape into a ball. Refrigerate. Serve with crackers.

SMOKY CHIPOTLE TROUT PATE

2 fillets smoked trout, flaked
3/4 C. unsalted butter, softened
5 oz. cream cheese, softened
4 oz. mild goat cheese, softened
1 t. chipotle en adobo, minced

2 T. freshly-squeezed lime juice
1 large scallion, chopped fine
2 T. fresh cilantro, chopped
Salt and pepper, to taste

Beat the butter with the cheeses and chipotle chilies until well blended. Beat in the trout and lime juice by hand. Stir in the scallion and cilantro. Add the salt and pepper. Cover the bowl and refrigerate for several hours. When ready to serve, let set out at room temperature.

Life is too short to drink cheap wine.

Notes

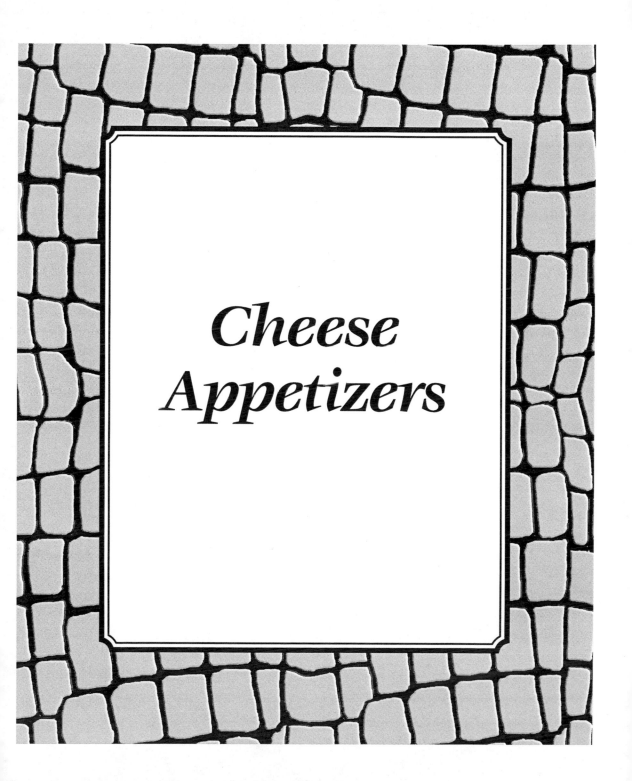

Cheese Appetizers

GOAT CHEESE WITH SUN-DRIED TOMATOES

Sun-dried tomato halves, not
  packed in oil
1 clove garlic, finely chopped
1 T. chopped fresh or dried
  rosemary

3 T. olive oil
1-10 oz. pkg. goat cheese
Fresh rosemary sprigs

Cover tomato halves with boiling water in a small bowl; let stand 5 minutes. Drain and chop tomatoes. Combine tomato, garlic, rosemary and oil in a small bowl. Cover and refrigerate up to 4 hours. Place goat cheese on a serving plate and let stand until room temperature. Pour tomato mixture over goat cheese. Garnish with rosemary. Serve with crackers or toasted baguette slices brushed with olive oil. Makes 6 to 8 servings.

BAKED GOAT CHEESE

1/2 t. cracked black pepper
1/4 t. dried thyme
1/4 t. fennel seeds
1/4 t. paprika
1/8 t. dried rosemary

1/8 t. ground red pepper
1/4 C. plain dried bread crumbs
2 T. extra-virgin oil
11 to 12 oz. plain goat cheese

Prepare crumb topping: With mortar and pestle, crush black pepper with thyme, fennel, paprika, rosemary and ground red pepper. In small bowl, toss herb mixture with bread crumbs and olive oil. Store in airtight container until ready to use. Preheat broiler. Evenly crumble goat cheese into shallow 8-inch round gratin dish. Sprinkle crumb mixture over goat cheese. With oven rack 5 to 7 inches from source of heat, broil goat-cheese mixture 2 to 3 minutes, until crumb topping is lightly browned. Garnish with thyme sprig. Makes 12 servings.

ROQUEFORT CHEESE BALL

3/4 lb. Roquefort cheese, at room
  temperature
1/2 lb. cream cheese, at room
  temperature

3 T. brandy
2 C. finely-chopped walnuts or
  toasted pecans

Using an electric mixer, beat the Roquefort cheese until creamy. Add the cream cheese and continue beating until smooth. Mix in the brandy. Divide the mixture in half. Place each half on a sheet of plastic wrap and form them into 2 roughly shaped logs, 1 1/2- to 2-inches in diameter. Wrap tightly and refrigerate until firm, at least an hour. When they are firm enough, roll each wrapped log back and forth on the counter to shape a more perfect log. Unwrap and roll in the nuts. Once again wrap tightly and refrigerate for at least several hours. Serve at room temperature either whole as a spread or sliced into rounds to put atop crackers or bread, or spread the mixture on crackers or bread, pop under the broiler a few minutes, and serve warm. Makes about 24 rounds.

HOLIDAY CHEESE BALL

1 small can chopped black olives
Bunch green onions or chives,
  finely chopped
1 C. butter, softened

1 lb. cream cheese, softened
2-4 oz. pkg. blue cheese, crumbled
1 C. chopped nuts

Combine butter, cream cheese and blue cheese. Mix together olives and chopped green onions. Form into balls and roll in chopped nuts. Chill and serve.

CHEESE ROLL

2-8 oz. pkg. cream cheese, softened
1 C. sharp Cheddar cheese, grated
1 avocado, mashed
1 onion, finely minced

1/2 C. pecans, finely chopped
1 t. garlic powder
1-4 oz. can green chilies, chopped
Salt, to taste

Blend the two cheeses. Add the rest of the ingredients and mix well. Divide into 2, and form into 2 rolls. Coat it with red chili powder. Wrap in waxed paper and refrigerate overnight. Slice and serve with crackers.

QUESADILLAS WITH CREAMY SALSA

8- 8-inch flour tortillas
1 C. shredded reduced-fat
  Cheddar cheese

1 C. shredded fat-free Monterey
  Jack cheese
1/2 C. canned chopped green
  chilies, drained

Yogurt Salsa:
3/4 C. plain nonfat yogurt
1/4 C. chopped tomato
1/4 C. chopped onion

2 t. minced fresh cilantro
1/2 t. lemon juice

Combine all yogurt salsa ingredients in a small bowl and mix well. Cover and refrigerate for at least 2 hours. Preheat oven to 350 degrees F. Divide cheese and green chilies evenly between 4 of the tortillas. Top with the remaining 4 tortillas. Coat a large baking sheet with aluminum foil. Place tortillas on baking sheet and bake until crispy and cheese melts, about 10 minutes. Slice each tortilla into 8 wedges and serve with yogurt salsa. Makes 8 servings. Yields approximately 1 cup.

FIESTA CREAM CHEESE

1-8 oz. pkg. fat-free cream cheese
1/2 C. salsa
1 T. fresh cilantro, chopped

1 T. fat-free Cheddar cheese, finely
  shredded
1 T. ripe olives, sliced
Assorted crackers

Place block of cream cheese on plate and leave unrefrigerated to soften.
Pour salsa over cream cheese, sprinkle with cilantro, cheese and olives.
Serve with crackers. Makes 8 servings.

CHILI CHEESECAKE

Pat Snyder, Dallas, TX.

1 C. crushed tortilla chips
3 T. melted butter
2-8 oz. pkg. softened cream cheese
2 eggs, beaten
1 fresh jalapeño pepper, cored,
  seeded and diced
1-4 oz. can diced green chilies
4 oz. shredded Colby cheese

4 oz. shredded Monterey Jack
  cheese
1/2 C. sour cream
Chopped tomatoes
Chopped green onions
Diced black olives
Sliced avocados

Mix the chips and butter and press into bottom of 9-inch springform
pan. Preheat oven to 325 degrees F. and bake 15 minutes. Leave the oven
on. Mix the cream cheese and eggs. Add the cheeses, green chilies and
jalapeño. Pour into the crust and bake 30 minutes. Remove from oven
and cool 5 minutes. Remove from the pan. Spread the sour cream over
the top and add the rest of the ingredients. Serve with tortilla chips.
Serves 10 to 12.

CHILI CHEESE SQUARES

6 eggs, beaten
1 small can evaporated milk
2 small cans green chilies,
  chopped

1 lb. Monterey Jack cheese
1 lb. sharp Cheddar cheese

Add evaporated milk to eggs and mix. Place in a 9x13-inch buttered Pyrex pan. Lay green chilies on top of mixture. Cover with cheese mixture. Bake at 350 degrees F. for 40 minutes. Do not cover while baking. When cool, cut into 1-inch squares and warm before serving. Freezes well.

JALAPEÑO SQUARES

1 lb. Monterey Jack cheese, grated
1 lb. Cheddar cheese, grated
1/2 C. finely-chopped jalapeño
  peppers

2 eggs
1 C. flour
1-12 oz. can evaporated milk

Arrange cheeses that have been mixed together with chopped peppers in ungreased 9x13-inch ovenproof dish. Mix eggs, flour and evaporated milk and pour over cheese mixture. Bake in preheated oven at 350 degrees F. for 40 minutes. Makes 48 squares.

TORTILLA ROLL-UPS

16 oz. softened cream cheese
1/4 C. mayonnaise
1/4 C. sour cream
1 packet dry ranch dressing mix
1-2.8 oz. pkg. Oscar Mayer real
  bacon pieces, or 5 slices
  crumbled cooked bacon

2-10 oz. pkg. frozen chopped
  spinach, thawed, drained and
  squeezed very dry
Flour tortillas

In a medium bowl, combine all ingredients, except the tortillas. Spread generously on flour tortillas. Roll up, wrap in plastic wrap and chill. Slice into approximately 3/4-inch slices. Place on plate cut-side up, to display the pretty layers.

REUBEN ROLL-UPS

2-8 oz. pkg. crescent rolls
1-2.5 oz. pkg. corned beef,
  chopped

1/2 can sauerkraut, drained and
  chopped
1/4 C. Thousand Island dressing
1 C. finely-shredded Swiss cheese

Spread about 1 1/2 teaspoons dressing evenly on each triangle, top with a little bit of corned beef, sauerkraut and cheese. Roll up starting at the shortest side, seal. Cut each roll into 4 slices and place them cut-side down on baking sheet. Bake at 375 degrees F. about 20 to 22 minutes.

PIMIENTO CHEESE

2 lbs. sharp Cheddar cheese,
  grated coarsely
3 hard-boiled eggs, grated coarse
1 large onion, grated coarse
2-7 oz. cans whole pimientos,
  chopped coarse, with their juice
2 C. mayonnaise
3 T. prepared mustard

3 T. Worcestershire sauce
2 t. salt
1/2 t. freshly-ground black pepper
1/2 t. paprika
1/2 t. onion salt
1/2 t. garlic salt
1/2 t. celery salt

Stir all ingredients in your largest mixing bowl until just well mixed. Do not mash or pack down, the mixture should be coarse and loose. It will become firmer when chilled. It keeps well when refrigerated, about 3 weeks. Do not freeze. Makes 2 quarts.

FRIED CHEDDAR CHEESE

1 1/4 C. fine, dry bread crumbs
1 T. sesame seeds
1-10 oz. pkg. sharp Cheddar
  cheese, cut into 1/2-inch cubes

2 eggs, beaten
Vegetable oil

Combine bread crumbs and sesame seeds in a shallow dish. Dip cheese cubes in beaten egg and dredge in crumb mixture. Repeat procedure. Place cheese on wax paper and chill 1 hour. Pour oil to a depth of 2 inches into a Dutch oven. Heat to 375 degrees F. Fry cheese in hot oil until golden brown. Drain on paper towels. Serve immediately. Makes 2 dozen.

CHEESE SHORTIES

1 lb. extra-sharp white Cheddar
  cheese, grated
1/2 lb. unsalted butter, softened

2 C. flour
Few dashes cayenne pepper

Cream the cheese and butter until thoroughly mixed, using an electric mixer or food processor. Add the flour and cayenne and mix thoroughly. Shape into rolls 1-inch in diameter, wrap in wax paper or plastic wrap and chill at least 1 hour or overnight, or freeze. If freezing, wrap again with aluminum foil. To serve, preheat the oven to 400 degrees F. If frozen, let the rolls defrost in the refrigerator for at least a couple of hours or overnight. Cut into 1/3-inch-thick slices and place on cookie sheets 1 inch apart. Bake for about 10 minutes, until light brown on the bottom. Makes 48 shorties.

ROQUEFORT PECAN LOG

2-3 oz. pkg. cream cheese, softened
8 oz. Roquefort cheese, crumbled
2 T. grated onion

1 small clove garlic, crushed
1 C. chopped pecans

Combine first 4 ingredients in a mixing bowl. Beat at medium speed of an electric mixer until smooth. Shape mixture into a 10-inch log and roll in chopped pecans. Cover and chill at least 3 hours. Serve with assorted crackers. Makes about 2 cups.

CHUTNEY BAKED BRIE

1-8-inch round brie cheese
1 C. chutney, finely chopped
1/2 lb. bacon, cooked and
  crumbled

1/4 C. green onion, including tops,
  minced
Your choice of crackers

Place brie in a 10-inch ovenproof dish or quiche dish and spread chutney to within one inch of edge. Top with crumbled bacon. Bake in a preheated 350 degree F. oven for 30 to 40 minutes, or until bubbly. Remove from oven and top with green onions. Serve hot brie with crackers. Serves 16-20.

BAKED BRIE

1 brick-sized chunk brie cheese
1 can Pillsbury crescent rolls

3 apples, sliced, 2 red and 1 green

Remove crescent rolls from can and spread out on a greased cookie sheet or an ovenproof serving platter. Press rolls together to form a large rectangle, making sure that all seams are sealed well. Place cheese in the center of dough. Wrap the dough around the cheese brick until it is completely covered. Bake at 375 degrees F. for 20 to 25 minutes, or until golden brown. A knife inserted in center should not stick, but come out easily. Serve on a platter surrounded with apple slices.

FIESTA BRIE

Leslie Updike, Chandler, AZ.

1 Brie round   Pineapple salsa (see following
                                       recipe)

Slice Brie in half horizontally. Scoop out Brie from bottom half to make a shallow saucer. Spoon salsa onto bottom half. Replace top inserting toothpicks to hold. Microwave 35 seconds. Remove toothpicks. Serve with bread slices.

PINEAPPLE SALSA

8 oz. mild salsa   1 C. cilantro, chopped
1 tomato, chopped   1 green onion, chopped
1/2 C. crushed pineapple, drained

Combine. Refrigerate one hour before serving.

When did my wild oats turn into shredded wheat?

MEXICAN BAKED BRIE

1-8-inch round of Brie
1 banana
1 1/2 C. orange marmalade
Cilantro
Jalapeños

Almonds
1/4 C. Grand Marnier
Puff pastry sheet
1 egg

Slice banana very thinly. De-seed and chop jalapeño. Chop cilantro leaves. Toast almonds until golden. In a saucepan, combine marmalade and Grand Marnier and cook until bubbly. Set aside 1/4 cup of mixture. Add jalapeños to remaining mixture and sauté until soft. Add cilantro and sauté approximately one minute. Remove from heat. Slice Brie down the middle, horizontally and place banana slices and small amount of orange mixture on top of bottom half. Top with other half of brie. Place pastry on oven safe platter and add remaining bananas, orange mixture and toasted almonds. Top with brie. Wrap pastry in a blanket form and turn over. Vent the brie and brush with beaten egg yolk. Bake at 350 degrees F. until bubbly and golden brown. Let set for at least 10 minutes. Drizzle with remaining orange mixture. Garnish with mandarin orange slices and orange spirals. Serve with crisp, salty crackers.

Does wine count as a serving of fruit?

HOT BAKED BRIE

2-4 oz. pkg. refrigerated crescent
  roll dough
8 oz. Brie cheese wheel

2 T. Tabasco red/green pepper
  sauce

Preheat oven to 375 degrees F. Work crescent roll dough into a thin circle large enough to completely wrap the brie. Place Brie in center of dough circle. With fork, poke top of cheese several times. Slowly pour 1 tablespoon Tabasco red/green pepper sauce over top of cheese, allowing it to sink in. Add remaining Tabasco sauce, poking cheese a few more times with fork, some sauce will run over side of cheese. Fold dough over top of cheese, working it together. Brush edges with beaten egg to hold seal. Bake approximately 10 minutes, following directions on crescent roll package. Do not overbake, as cheese will run. Serve immediately with crackers. Serves 10.

GREEN CHILI WON TONS

Won Tons:
1/2 lb. Monterey Jack cheese,
  grated
1-4 oz. can green chilies, chopped

1-14 oz. pkg. won ton skins
Vegetable oil

Guacamole Dip:
2 large ripe avocados
3 T. fresh lime juice
1/2 t. salt

1/2 t. ground coriander
2 t. minced green onions
3 T. mayonnaise

Mix cheese and green chilies. Place 1 tablespoon on a won ton skin and fold like an envelope. Fry in 2 inches of hot oil until brown, turning so that both sides will be brown. Drain. Serve with guacamole dip.

Guacamole Dip: Mash pulp of avocados and blend in lime juice. Add remaining ingredients and blend until smooth. Cover and refrigerate until ready to use. Can be frozen ahead. Makes 6-10 servings.

MEXICAN PINWHEELS

3-8 oz. pkg. cream cheese, softened
1-8 oz. carton sour cream
1/2 t. garlic powder
1-4 oz. can green chilies, chopped
1-4 oz. can black olives, drained
  and chopped

1/2 C. chives, chopped
Juice of one lime
1/4 C. picante sauce
36 taco-sized flour tortillas

In a medium bowl, combine the first 8 ingredients. Divide among 36 flour tortillas and spread out. Roll tortillas into logs and refrigerate overnight. It is best if they are refrigerated overnight. But, if you do not have that long, at least refrigerate them for a few hours to help them hold together better. To serve, slice logs into bite-sized pieces. These freeze well. Serve with picante sauce for dipping.

BLUE CHEESE PUFFS

2-8 oz. pkg. cream cheese, softened
1 C. mayonnaise
1 T. minced onions
1/4 C. minced fresh chives
3/4 to 1 C. blue cheese, crumbled

1/2 t. cayenne pepper
1 loaf whole wheat bread, very
  thinly sliced
Paprika

Mix cream cheese and mayonnaise in a medium bowl. Stir in onions, chives, blue cheese and cayenne pepper. Set aside. Using a 1 1/2- to 2-inch round cookie cutter, cut bread slices into rounds. Spread 1 tablespoon of cheese mixture on each round. Place puffs on a baking sheet and freeze. When ready to serve, preheat oven to 350 degrees F. Remove baking sheet from freezer. Bake 15 minutes. Sprinkle with paprika. Serve immediately. Makes 60 puffs.

JALAPEÑO FUDGE

1 lb. Monterey Jack cheese,
  shredded
1 lb. Cheddar cheese, shredded
1/2 c. chopped canned jalapeño
  chilies
1/2 C. chopped green onions

2 eggs
1 C. flour
3-5 oz. cans evaporated milk
1 t. cumin
Salt and pepper, to taste

Toss the Monterey Jack cheese and Cheddar cheese in a bowl. Spread in a 9x13-inch baking dish. Sprinkle with the jalapeño chilies and green onions. Whisk the eggs in a bowl until blended. Add the flour and whisk until smooth. Add the evaporated milk gradually, whisking constantly until blended. Stir in the cumin, salt and pepper. Pour the egg mixture over the cheese. Bake at 350 degrees F. for 40 minutes. Let stand until cool. Cut into bite-size squares. Makes 3 to 4 dozen squares.

PHYLLO FETA WRAPS

1 lb. Feta cheese, in one piece
5 T. unsalted butter, melted

6 sheets phyllo dough

Preheat oven to 375 degrees F. Portion cheese into 24 sticks by cutting piece in half horizontally, then into rectangles that are 2 1/2-inches long and 1/2-inch wide. Cut phyllo sheets into 4 equal pieces. Brush lightly with butter. Roll 1 piece of cheese in 1 piece of phyllo, tucking sides and flaps underneath. Brush with additional butter. Place on baking sheet. Bake for 10 to 15 minutes, until golden brown. Serve on colorful platter. Makes 24 wraps.

TEXAS TORTILLAS

1-8 oz. pkg. cream cheese, softened
1-8 oz. carton sour cream
5 scallions with tops, chopped
   fine, or 1 small onion, minced
3 jalapeño peppers, seeded and
   chopped fine, or 4 oz. can
   chopped green chilies

2 T. chopped black olives
1/2 C. sharp Cheddar cheese,
   shredded
1-12 count pkg. large flour tortillas
Picante sauce

Place the cream cheese, sour cream, scallions, jalapeños, olives and cheese in a food processor. Process until smooth. Spread the mixture on flour tortillas and roll up. Wrap the tortillas in damp paper towels and place in plastic storage bags. Chill. To serve, cut tortillas into 1-inch pieces. Place on a tray with a bowl of picante sauce and toothpicks. Makes 5 dozen.

"You'd be surprised how much it costs to look this cheap." Dolly Parton

SALSA CHEESE BAKE

2 cloves garlic, finely chopped
1 T. vegetable oil
1-12 oz. jar salsa
1-4 oz. can chopped green chilies, drained
2 T. raisins
1/4 t. ground cinnamon
1/8 t. ground cloves

Dash of ground cumin
1/2 lb. bulk Italian sausage
16 oz. Monterey Jack cheese, cut into 1/4-inch slices
1/4 C. sliced pimento-stuffed olives
1-12 oz. pkg. round tortilla chips

Cook and stir garlic in oil in 1-quart saucepan until garlic is brown, about 1 minute. Stir in salsa, chilies, raisins, cinnamon, cloves and cumin. Heat to boiling, stirring occasionally. Reduce heat. Simmer, uncovered, stirring occasionally, until mixture is slightly thickened, about 3 minutes. Cook and stir sausage in 10-inch skillet until brown. Drain. Stir in 1 cup of the salsa mixture. Place half of the cheese slices in single layer in ungreased 1-quart shallow casserole or pie plate, 9 x 1 1/4-inches. Spoon sausage mixture over cheese slices in casserole and top with remaining cheese slices. Bake, uncovered, in 400 degree F. oven until cheese is melted, 8 to 10 minutes. Heat remaining salsa mixture and the olives until hot and pour over cheese. Serve with tortilla chips. Makes 15.

Whatever hits the fan will not be evenly distributed.

CHILI QUICHE APPETIZERS

1-4 oz. can whole green chilies,
    drained, seeded and chopped
2 C. shredded Monterey Jack or
    Cheddar cheese

1 C. variety baking mix
1 C. half-and-half
4 eggs
1/8 t. red pepper sauce, if desired

Heat oven to 375 degrees F. Grease square pan, 9x9x2-inches. Sprinkle chilies and cheese in pan. Beat remaining ingredients until smooth, 15 seconds in blender on high speed or 1 minute with hand beater. Pour into pan. Bake until golden brown and knife inserted in center comes out clean, about 30 minutes. Let stand 10 minutes before cutting. Cut into about 1 1/4-inch squares. Refrigerate any remaining appetizers. Makes 3 dozen.

SOUTHERN CHEESE BALL

3-8 oz. pkg. cream cheese, softened
1 C. crushed pineapple, well
    drained

5 green onions, finely chopped
1/2 green pepper, chopped
1/2 C. pecans, finely chopped

Mix all the ingredients, except the pecans, and shape into a ball. Roll in the pecans.

We'll drink no wine before it's time. It's time!

CHILI-CHEESE BALLS

1-4 oz. can chopped green chilies, well drained
2 C. shredded Cheddar cheese
1 C. flour

1/2 C. margarine or butter, softened
1/2 t. salt

Heat oven to 375 degrees F. Mix all ingredients. Shape into 3/4-inch balls. Place about 2 inches apart on greased cookie sheet. Bake until set, 15 to 18 minutes. Makes 6 dozen.

BLUE CHEESE AND BRANDY CHEESE BALL

2 C. shredded Cheddar cheese
1-8 oz. pkg. cream cheese
1/2 C. crumbled blue cheese
3 T. brandy
2 T. finely-chopped onion
1 T. Worcestershire sauce

Dash bottled hot pepper sauce
Dash garlic powder
1/4 C. snipped parsley
1/4 C. finely-chopped toasted almonds
Assorted crackers

Bring Cheddar cheese, cream cheese and blue cheese to room temperature. In a mixer bowl, beat cheeses, brandy, onion, Worcestershire sauce, hot pepper sauce and garlic powder together with an electric mixer until combined. Cover and chill for several hours or overnight. Before serving, shape cheese mixture into a ball. Combine parsley and almonds. Roll cheese ball in the parsley-almond mixture. Serve with crackers. Makes 1 ball.

PITA CHEESE CRISPS

2/3 C. grated Romano or Parmesan
  cheese
4 C. grated Cheddar cheese
12 T. unsalted butter, softened
1 clove garlic, minced

3/4 t. Worcestershire sauce
1 t. paprika
1/4 t. ground red pepper
6 large pita breads

Preheat oven to 350 degrees F. In a large mixing bowl or food processor, combine the cheeses, butter, garlic, Worcestershire sauce, paprika and cayenne pepper. Split the pita breads into 2 flat disks. Spread with cheese mixture and cut into small wedges with a serrated knife. Place the wedges 1/2-inch apart on an ungreased cookie sheet. Bake for 10 to 12 minutes and serve warm. These may be made ahead and frozen before baking. Makes about 60 wedges.

Work like you don't need money.
Love like you've never been hurt.
Dance like nobody's watching.

COWBOY CRISP

1 3/4 C. flour
1/2 C. yellow cornmeal
1/2 t. baking soda
1/2 t. sugar
1/2 t. salt
1/2 C. butter

8 oz. extra-sharp Cheddar cheese,
  shredded
2 T. white vinegar
2/3 C. water
Coarsely-ground black pepper

In large bowl, combine flour, cornmeal, baking soda, sugar and salt. With pastry blender or 2 knives, cut in butter until mixture resembles coarse crumbs. With fork, stir in cheese, vinegar and water just until mixture forms a soft dough. Divide into 4 equal pieces, wrap in plastic wrap and chill 1 hour. May be chilled in freezer about 30 minutes. Preheat oven to 375 degrees F. Grease large baking sheet. On lightly-floured surface, with floured rolling pin, roll 1 piece of dough into paper-thin 10-inch circle. Edges may be ragged. Cut into 8 wedges and place on prepared baking sheet. Sprinkle wedges with coarsely-ground black pepper firmly pressing pepper into dough. Bake about 10 minutes, or until browned and crisp. Remove from oven and transfer crisp to racks and cool. Repeat with remaining dough. Store at room temperature in covered container. Serves 10-12.

What if the HOKEY POKEY is really what it's all about?

Fondue

SPICY CHICKEN FONDUE

6 boned and skinned chicken
  breasts
4 T. oil
2 t. paprika
1/2 t. chili powder
1 T. oil

1 onion, finely chopped
2 t. mild curry powder
3 t. flour
1 1/4 C. milk
6 t. mango chutney
Salt and pepper, to taste

Cut chicken into 3/4-inch pieces. Mix the 4 tablespoons of oil, paprika
and chili powder in a skillet. Cook the chicken in the hot oil mixture and
cook until done. Heat the 1 tablespoon oil in a saucepan. Add the onion
and cook until soft. Stir in the curry powder and cook for 2 minutes, then
stir in the flour. Gradually stir in the milk and bring slowly to a bowl
stirring all the time. Continue to cook until sauce thickens. Simmer for 5
minutes. Add the chutney and season with the salt and pepper. Add the
chicken and put in a fondue pot.

Wine a little. You'll feel better!

TEXAS FONDUE

1 round loaf of bread
2 T. vegetable oil
1 T. butter, melted
1 1/2 C. sour cream
1-8 oz. sharp Cheddar cheese,
  grated

1-8 oz. pkg. cream cheese, softened
1 C. ham, diced and cooked
1/2 C. green onions, chopped
1-4 oz. can green chilies, drained
  and chopped
1 t. Worcestershire sauce

Preheat oven to 350 degrees F. Slice off the top of the bread and set aside. Hollow out the insides with a small paring knife, leaving a half inch shell. Cut removed bread into 1-inch cubes. In a large skillet, combine oil and butter. Add the bread cubes and stir until thoroughly coated. Place on a cookie sheet. Bake for 10 to 15 minutes turning occasionally, until golden brown. Remove from oven and reserve to serve with the fondue. Mix all the rest of the ingredients and spoon the mixture into the hollow bread, filling it. Replace the top of the bread and wrap in heavy-duty foil. Set loaf on a cookie sheet. Bake for 1 hour and 10 minutes. When bread is done, remove the wrap and place on a serving dish and serve with the bread cubes.

SWEET AND SOUR FONDUE

1 lb. bulk pork sausage
2-5 oz. pkg. party-size smoked
  sausage links
1-20 oz. can pineapple chunks,
  drained, saving the juice

1 jar maraschino cherries, drained
3 T. honey
3 T. vinegar
1 T. soy sauce
2 T. cornstarch

Shape the bulk sausage into balls. Brown balls and links in skillet. Drain. Reserve 2 tablespoons drippings. Place the juice of the pineapple in a fondue pot. Add the honey, vinegar, soy sauce and cornstarch. Blend until smooth. Add 2 tablespoons of the pan drippings. Bring to a boil, stirring constantly. Add the sausage, pineapple and cherries. Simmer for 15 minutes. Serve warm.

BEER CHEESE FONDUE

1 clove garlic, peeled
1-12 oz. can flat beer
3 T. flour
1/4 t. black pepper
1 dash Tabasco sauce

1/2 t. salt
1/2 t. ground mustard seed
1 lb. Cheddar cheese, grated
1 loaf French bread, cubed

Rub the garlic clove over the inside of the surface of a fondue pot. Mince garlic and set aside. In a saucepan, stir the beer and flour and form a paste. Add the remaining ingredients, except cheese. Heat over medium heat. Slowly add the cheese, stirring until cheese has melted. Pour into the fondue pot. Serve with the bread cubes.

CHILI FONDUE

2 C. Pepper Jack cheese, shredded
2 C. white Cheddar cheese, shredded
2 T. + 1 1/2 t. cornstarch
1 t. minced garlic
1 1/2 C. chicken broth

6 T. lemon juice
1/4 t. dried oregano
1/4 T. cumin
1 bunch scallions, thinly sliced
2 T. ripe black olives, chopped

Toss the cheeses with the cornstarch. In a saucepan, heat the broth, lemon juice, garlic, oregano and cumin until barely simmering. Add the cheeses, a handful at a time, stirring until the cheeses melt. Stir in the scallions and olives. Pour into a fondue pot.

LOBSTER FONDUE

2 T. butter
2 C. American cheese, shredded
2 drops red pepper sauce

1/3 C. dry white wine
1-5 oz. can lobster, drained and
   broken in small pieces

In the fondue pot, melt butter over low heat. Gradually stir in cheese until melted. Add the pepper sauce, gradually stir in wine. Add the lobster, stir until heated through. Makes about 1 1/2 cups.

HOT CRAB FONDUE

1-5 oz. jar American cheese
1-8 oz. pkg. cream cheese
1 can crab, drained
1/4 C. half and half
1/2 t. Worcestershire sauce

1/4 t. garlic powder
1/2 t. cayenne pepper
Fresh bread, cut into bite size
   cubes

Combine the cheeses over low heat in double boiler. Stir constantly until smooth. Add the rest of the remaining ingredients and mix well. Serve warm with bread cubes.

We only drink the finest California wines. Did you bring some?

CHEESE FONDUE

3 cans Cheddar cheese soup   1 t. garlic salt
1/2 C. white wine

Place all ingredients in a fondue pot and heat until the cheese melts. Use bread cubes to dip.

SHRIMP FONDUE

1 can condensed cream of shrimp   1 1/2 T. sherry
  soup   1/4 onion, finely chopped
1 C. milk   1/4 t. dry mustard
2 C. Swiss cheese, shredded

Add all the ingredients to a fondue pot and cook until cheese has melted. Use bread for dipping.

You call me Bitch like it's a bad thing!

MEXICAN FONDUE

2 lbs. Velveeta cheese
2-7 oz. cans green chili salsa

1-4 oz. can diced green chilies
1 envelope taco seasoning mix

Melt the cheese in a fondue pot. Add the rest of the ingredients. Let them blend for 30 minutes. Use bread cubes to dip.

CHEESE AND WILD MUSHROOM FONDUE

1 1/2 t. olive oil
4 oz. fresh shiitake mushrooms,
  stemmed, caps diced
1 shallot, minced
1 t. fresh thyme, chopped
1 1/2 T. flour

12 oz. chilled double cream brie
  cheese
2 oz. chilled Roquefort cheese
1 C. dry white wine
Black pepper, to taste

Sauté the mushrooms, shallot and thyme in the oil over medium-high heat for 2 minutes. Cut the rind off the brie and discard. Cut into cubes. Add the flour to a bowl, and coat the brie cubes. Toss to cover. Crumble the Roquefort into the same bowl and toss to cover. In a heavy medium saucepan, bring to a simmer over medium heat. Add the cheese, stirring until melted. Continue stirring until smooth. Stir the mushroom mixture into the wine. Add the black pepper and transfer to a fondue pot. Serve with bread cubes.

Some days are a total waste of make-up.

CARAMEL-PECAN FONDUE

1/3 C. butter
1/3 C. sugar
1/2 C. dark brown sugar
2/3 C. corn syrup

1 1/2 C. heavy cream
3 T. rum
1/3 C. pecans, finely chopped and
    divided

In a saucepan, warm the butter, sugars and corn syrup until the butter has melted. Increase the heat to medium-high and bring to a low boil. Let it boil, stirring occasionally, for 5 minutes. Add the cream, heat and stir for another 5 minutes. Stir in the rum and pecans, saving 1 tablespoon of the nuts. Transfer to a warm fondue pot and sprinkle with the remaining pecans. This is good to dip angel-food cake, marshmallows or any fruit.

FLAMING TURTLE CHOCOLATE FONDUE

1/4 C. milk
1/2 C. milk chocolate
1/4 C. caramel syrup

2 T. pecans, chopped
2 T. rum, 151-proof

Soften milk chocolate in the microwave. Heat the milk in the fondue pot. Add the chocolate and stir until it is smooth. Pour the caramel into a pool in the middle of the chocolate. When it is time to serve, pour the rum over the top of the chocolate. Leave a small amount on the spoon to ignite with a lighter. Use the flaming spoon to ignite the rum. Add the pecans. Allow the flame to burn out. Dip with fruits, marshmallows or cake, cubed.

CHOCOLATE FONDUE

4 oz. butter
4 oz. margarine
1.5 oz. unsweetened chocolate
1 t. vanilla extract
1 can evaporated milk

4 oz. condensed milk
2 lbs. confectioners' sugar
2 C. raspberries, frozen, puréed
1 ripe banana, puréed

In the top of a double boiler, place the first 3 ingredients and let melt. When the butter has melted, stir in the milks and let cook for 10 minutes. Place the sugar in a sifter and whisk in the chocolate, stirring until well mixed. Stirring the raspberries, banana and vanilla. Cook for 10 more minutes. Stir well. Use fresh fruit for dipping.

This is not the life I ordered!

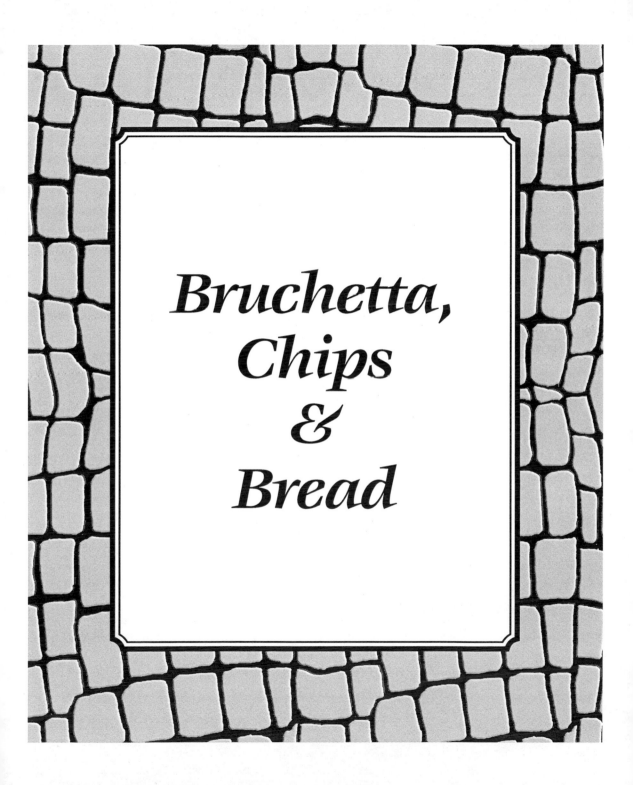

Bruchetta, Chips & Bread

B. L. T. BRUSCHETTA

8 to 10 slices bacon, crispy cooked
and crumbled
3 to 4 Roma tomatoes, seeded and
chopped
1 C. chopped leafy green lettuce
2 T. chopped fresh basil leaves
1 clove garlic, minced

1/4 t. salt
1/4 t. ground pepper
1/3 C. olive oil
1/2-16 oz. pkg. twin French bread
loaves, cut in 1/4-inch slices
1/3 C. favorite crumble cheese,
blue cheese or Feta

In medium bowl, stir together all topping ingredients; set aside. Brush olive oil on both sides of bread slices and place on baking sheet. Bake at 400 degrees F., turning once, for 7 minutes per side or until crisp and golden brown. Cool. Spoon about 1 tablespoon topping on each toast round. Makes about 24.

MUSHROOM BRUSCHETTA

6 mushrooms, thinly sliced
1 T. butter
1/4 C. butter, softened
4 cloves garlic, minced
1/2 t. garlic powder

6 1/2-inch slices Italian bread
6 slices Fontina cheese, trimmed to
fit bread slices
Extra-virgin oil
Julienne fresh basil

Sauté the mushrooms in the 1 tablespoon butter and drain. Mix 1/4 cup butter with the garlic and garlic powder. Spread butter mixture over the bread. Place a slice of the cheese on each piece of bread. Spoon the mushrooms over each slice. Preheat oven to 500 degrees F. Bake for 4 minutes or until cheese is melted. Remover from the oven and drizzle the olive oil over the bread. Sprinkle basil over the top.

BRUSCHETTA WITH FRESH TOMATOES AND GARLIC

1.5 lbs. ripe tomatoes
Sliced Italian bread, cut in 1/2-
  inch slices
Garlic clove, minced
2 T. capers, rinsed

1/4 C. loosely-packed fresh
  oregano
Salt and pepper, to taste
1/3 C. extra-virgin olive oil

Cut a cross at the root end of the tomatoes and drop in a saucepan of boiling water. Cook until the skin of the tomatoes begin to split, 1 to 2 minutes. Transfer the tomatoes to a bowl of iced water. Peel and seed the tomatoes, then roughly chop. Place in a strainer over a bowl for 30 minutes. Brush bread lightly with the olive oil and place under a broiler until golden on each side. Place the tomatoes, garlic, capers and oregano in a bowl. Season with the salt and pepper. Spoon over each piece of bread.

BRUSCHETTA WITH ROASTED PEPPERS

2 medium red bell peppers,
  roasted and peeled
2 garlic cloves, minced
2 anchovy fillets, chopped
1/4 C. extra-virgin olive oil

1 T. chopped parsley
Salt and pepper, to taste
2 slices Italian bread, cut 1/2-inch
  thick

Cut the bell peppers into 1/2-inch slices and place in a bowl. In a small bowl, add the garlic and anchovies with the olive oil and mix. Pour over the peppers. Add the parsley, salt and pepper. Brush the slices of bread with olive oil and broil until golden on both sides. Top with the pepper mixture.

BLUE CHEESE BRUSCHETTA

2 T. olive oil
2 onions, coarsely chopped
1 T. brown sugar
1 t. balsamic vinegar
1/2 t. salt

Dash white pepper
8 slices baguette bread, cut into
  1/4-inch thick pieces
1/3 C. crumbled blue cheese

Heat the oil in a large skillet. Cook the onions, brown sugar and vinegar about 25 minutes over medium heat, stirring frequently. When the onions are golden brown, remove from the heat and sprinkle with salt and pepper. Stir. Place the bread on an ungreased cookie sheet. Broil until lightly browned. Turn the bread over and spread the onion mixture over the bread and sprinkle with the cheese. Broil until cheese is melted.

WALNUT BRUSCHETTA

3 oz. Parmesan cheese, grated
1/2 C. chopped walnuts
1/4 t. salt

3/4 C. olive oil
1/2 loaf narrow French bread

Combine 1/2 cup cheese, 1/4 cup walnuts and salt in a food processor. Process until finely chopped. Add 1/4 cup oil and process until fairly smooth. Cut bread on the diagonal into 24-1/2-inch slices. Brush on both sides with remaining 1/2 cup of oil. Toast bread on baking sheet under the broiler, about 30 seconds on each side. Remove from oven and spread walnut mixture on each slice. Sprinkle with remaining cheese. Press remaining walnut on top. Broil until cheese begins to melt, about 30 seconds.

TRISCUIT BRUSCHETTA

1 C. plum tomatoes, chopped
1/4 C. Parmesan cheese, grated
1/4 C. green onions, chopped
2 T. fresh basil, chopped

2 T. Italian dressing
1/2 t. garlic, minced
36 Triscuit reduced-fat crackers

Preheat oven to 400 degrees F. Mix all ingredients, except Triscuits. Spoon mixture on the Triscuits. Place on a baking sheet and bake 5 to 7 minutes.

ARTICHOKE BRUSCHETTA

1-14-inch loaf Italian bread
1 C. canned artichoke hearts,
  drained and chopped
1 C. tomatoes, chopped
1/4 C. onion, finely chopped

3 cloves garlic, pressed
2 T. olive oil
1 1/2 T. balsamic vinegar
1/2 t. ground black pepper
Fresh grated Parmesan cheese

Preheat oven to 350 degrees F. Slice bread cross wise into 24-1/2-inch pieces. Bake for 10 minutes. Combine all the ingredients, except the Parmesan cheese. Spread over the bread. Sprinkle with cheese.

"Seize the moment! Remember all those women on the Titanic who waved off the dessert cart." Erma Bombeck

SPICY POTATO CHIPS

2 sweet potatoes, peeled and
   sliced 1/8-inch thick
2 Idaho potatoes, peeled and
   sliced 1/8-inch thick

Peanut oil for frying
3 T. Cajun or taco seasoning
1/2 C. blue cheese, crumbled
Tabasco sauce

Soak the sweet potatoes and Idaho potatoes in separate bowls of ice water in the refrigerator for 4 hours. Preheat the oven to 250 degrees F. Heat oil in a deep fryer to 370 degrees F. Drain the potatoes and pat dry with paper towels. Fry the potatoes in small batches until nicely browned. Bring the oil back to temperature before frying the next batch. Drain the chips on brown paper bags or paper towels and sprinkle with the Cajun or taco seasoning. As you finish each batch, place chips in a single layer on a baking sheet in the oven to keep warm and crisp. When all of the chips are fried, crumble the blue cheese on top and heat in the oven for 5 minutes, or until the cheese is soft. Serve with Tabasco sauce on the side. Serves 6.

SWEET POTATO CHIPS

1 large sweet potato, peeled
1/4 t. salt

Pam

Preheat oven to 325 degrees F. Cut the potato into 1/8-inch slices. Arrange in a single layer on baking sheets coated with Pam. Coat sweet potato slices with the Pam. Bake for 15 to 25 minutes, or until crisp. Cool. Sprinkle with salt. Makes 3 dozen.

PITA CHIPS

3 large pita breads
6 T. garlic oil

6 T. freshly-grated Parmesan
cheese

Preheat oven to 300 degrees F. Split pita breads horizontally to make 6 rounds. Brush each with garlic oil, sprinkle with cheese and cut into 8 triangles. Place on baking sheet. Bake for 15 minutes, or until crisp and golden. Cool and store in airtight container for up to 2 days. Makes 48 chips.

ROQUEFORT BISCUITS

8 oz. imported Roquefort cheese,
   at room temperature
1 stick unsalted butter

1 1/3 to 1 1/2 C. packed self-rising
   flour

Preheat oven to 350 degrees. Crumble Roquefort into bowl of electric mixer. Add butter, cut into small pieces, and mix for 1 minute until blended. Add a grinding of black pepper, flour and 1 to 2 tablespoons cold water. Mix on medium speed until dough comes away from sides of bowl. Do not overmix. Dough should be firm and not at all sticky. Add a little flour if necessary. Lightly dust a flat surface with flour and with your hands roll dough into a 1-inch diameter log. Slice into 1/2-inch thick rounds. Place rounds on ungreased baking sheet and bake for 20 minutes. Serve warm. These also freeze well and reheat beautifully. Makes 22 to 24 biscuits.

CHEDDAR SHORTBREAD

3/4 C. butter, softened
1/4 t. dry mustard
1/2 T. ground pepper

1 1/2 C. grated Cheddar cheese
1 1/4 C. flour
1 C. pecans, chopped

Preheat oven to 350 degrees F. Mix the butter, mustard and pepper in a food processor and blend. Add the cheese and whirl. Add flour and pulse just until blended. Roll the dough out on a flour surface. Roll to a 1/4-inch thickness. Cut with a small cookie cutter. Place on a cookie sheet and sprinkle with chopped pecans. Bake for 20 minutes.

FOCACCIA

2 pkg. fast-rising dry yeast
2 C. warm water
2 T. sugar
4 T. olive oil
1/2 C. salad oil
1 t. salt

5 1/2 C. flour
3 cloves garlic, crushed
1/4 C. olive oil, for the topping
1 T. rosemary, for topping
1 T. coarse sea salt, for topping

Dissolve the yeast in the water. Add the next 5 ingredients. Mix in 3 cups of flour and whip until the dough begins to leave the sides of the bowl, about 10 minutes. Add the rest of the flour by hand and knead the dough until it is smooth. Allow the dough to rise twice in the bowl, punching down after each rising. Oil two baking sheets and divide the dough between each pan. Using your fingers, press the dough out to the edges of each pan. Cover and allow to rise for about 30 minutes. Brush with the crushed garlic and oil. Sprinkle with rosemary and kosher salt. Bake in preheated oven 375 degrees F. for 30 minutes.

SEASONED CRACKERS

1-16 oz. bag oyster crackers
1/2 pkg. dry Hidden Valley Ranch
   dressing

3/4 C. vegetable oil

Mix all the ingredients in a bowl with a cover. Shake and let set 2 hours. Shake well again before serving.

Put on your girl panties and deal with it!

Misc.

CREAM CHEESE STRAWBERRIES

1-8 oz. pkg. cream cheese, softened
2 T. sugar
1 T. vanilla extract

16 large strawberries, trimmed
  and cored
Slivered almonds and fresh mint
  leaves, for garnish

Combine the cream cheese, sugar and vanilla extract in a small bowl. Beat well. Spoon the mixture into a pastry bag fitted with a star tip. Pipe into the strawberries. Garnish with almond slivers and fresh mint leaves. Makes 16.

ROQUEFORT GRAPES

1 lb. large, seedless red grapes,
  about 50 grapes
10 oz. pecans

4 T. crumbled Roquefort cheese
1-8 oz. pkg. cream cheese, softened
2 T. heavy cream

Wash the grapes and pat dry. Crush the pecans on a platter or sheet of waxed paper. Combine the Roquefort cheese, cream cheese and cream in a bowl and mix well. Roll the grapes in the cheese mixture and then in the pecans, coating well. Chill, covered, until serving time. Makes 50.

Nothing chocolate, nothing gained.

RANCH PECANS

1 C. water
1 C. sugar
3 to 4 dried red chilie peppers

2 C. pecan halves
1/4 C. molasses

Preheat oven to 250 degrees F. Combine water, sugar and chilies in a small saucepan. Bring to a boil. Add pecans and return to a boil. Reduce heat and simmer 10 minutes. Drain pecans. Transfer to a baking sheet. Bake 45 minutes, stirring occasionally. Pour pecans into a small bowl. Add molasses and toss to coat. Return pecans to the baking sheet. Bake an additional 45 minutes, or until pecans are very crisp, stirring occasionally. Makes 2 cups.

ROQUEFORT PECANS

3 oz. crumbled Roquefort cheese
1-3 oz. pkg. cream cheese, softened

120 pecan halves

Mix the cheeses until smooth. Then spread on flat side of a pecan half and press together, sandwich fashion. Makes 60.

*Men are like chocolates –
wait too long and only the weird nutty ones are left!*

BARBEQUE PECANS

2 T. butter
1/4 C. Worcestershire sauce
1 T. catsup

6 dashes hot sauce
4 C. pecan halves
Salt, to taste

Preheat oven to 400 degrees F. Melt the butter and add the next 3 ingredients. Stir in the pecans. Spoon into a glass baking dish, spreading evenly. Bake for 20 minutes, stirring frequently. Turn out on paper towels and salt.

SPICY PUMPKIN SEEDS

2 C. fresh pumpkin seeds, rinsed
  and dried
2 T. olive oil

1 t. salt
1 t. cayenne
1/2 t. cumin

Preheat oven to 350 degrees F. Mix all the ingredients, except the seeds. Toss with the seeds. Bake on a baking sheet for 30 to 45 minutes, tossing occasionally, until they are tan and crisp. Makes 2 cups.

Moms of teenagers know why animals eat their young!

CARAMEL CORN

3 qt. popped popcorn
3 C. unsalted mixed nuts
1 C. brown sugar, firmly packed
1/2 C. Karo light syrup

1 stick butter
1/2 t. salt
1/2 t. vanilla
1/2 t. baking soda

Preheat oven to 250 degrees F. Spray large shallow roasting pan with Pam. Mix popcorn and nuts in pan. Cook in oven while preparing syrup. In a large saucepan, mix the sugar, syrup, butter and salt. Over medium heat, stirring constantly, bring to a boil. Boil 5 minutes, without stirring. Remove from heat and stir in vanilla and soda. Pour over the warm popcorn mixture, stirring until the popcorn is coated thoroughly. Bake for 1 hour, stirring occasionally. Cook and break apart. Store in an airtight container.

NACHO POPCORN

1 t. paprika
1/2 t. crushed red-pepper
1/2 t. ground cumin

1/4 C. butter or margarine, melted
10 C. warm popped popcorn
1/3 C. grated Parmesan cheese

In a small bowl, stir paprika, red pepper and cumin into melted butter or margarine. Gently toss butter mixture with popcorn, coating evenly. Sprinkle with Parmesan cheese and toss until coated. Makes 10 cups.

I don't skinny dip, I chunky dunk!

PARMESAN-CURRY POPCORN

1/2 C. margarine or butter, melted
1/3 C. grated Parmesan cheese
1/2 t. salt

1/4 t. curry powder
12 C. popped corn

Mix margarine, cheese, salt and curry powder. Pour over popped corn and toss. Makes 12 cups.

FIRE MOUTH POPCORN

Leslie Updike, Chandler, AZ.

1 C. popping corn
2 jalapeño peppers, chopped
Salt

1/3 C. oil
1 t. turmeric
Cumin

In a large stockpot, heat oil and peppers on high for one-half minute. Add turmeric and corn. Remove from heat after the corn has popped, season with salt and cumin to taste.

If I knit fast, does it count as aerobic exercise?

TEXAS TRASH

3/4 C. bacon grease
1 1/2 sticks oleo
3 T. Worcestershire sauce
3 T. garlic salt
1 1/2 t. Accent
2 T. Tabasco sauce

1 large can mixed nuts
1/2 box Cheerios
2 boxes pretzels
1/2 box Wheat Chex
1/2 box Rice Chex
Oyster crackers (optional)

Melt first 6 ingredients in saucepan and pour over the next 6 ingredients. Bake 1 1/2 hours at 225 degrees F. Stir every 15 minutes. Place in coffee cans or covered containers and serve for snacks.

WHITE TRASH

1 C. Cheerios
1 C. Crispix
1 C. pretzel sticks

1 C. peanuts
1-12 oz. bag vanilla baking chips
1 T. vegetable oil

Melt the vanilla chips in microwave. Stir into the oil. Pour over the first 4 ingredients and stir to coat. Press onto waxed paper and allow to cool overnight. Break into pieces.

I understand the concepts of cooking and cleaning,
just not how they apply to me!

DOG FOOD

9 C. Chex cereal
6 oz. semi-sweet chocolate chips
1/2 C. peanut butter

1/4 C. butter
1 t. vanilla
1 1/2 C. powdered sugar

Microwave chocolate chips, peanut butter and butter in a bowl, uncovered, on HIGH, for 1 minute. Stir. Microwave 30 seconds longer, until mixture is smooth. Stir in the vanilla. Pour over the cereal and stir until mixture is coated. Store in Ziploc bags.

I have a life; it's on layaway at Neiman's!

Notes

INDEX

DIPS, SPREADS & SALSA

7 Layer Dip 10

Artichoke Salsa 34

Asparagus Dip 14

Avocado Lime Dip 15

B.L.T. Dip 8

Black Bean Dip 12

Black Bean Nacho Dip 11

Black-Eyed Pea Salsa 38

Blue Cheese and Caramelized Shallot Dip 21

Blue Crab Dip 3

Broccoli Dip 13

Cheese Spread 33

Cheese Wreath 23

Chicken Enchilada Dip 7

Chipotle Mayonnaise Dip with Carrots 21

Clam Dip 6

Coffee Fruit Dip 26

Corn and Tomato Salsa 34

Corn Salsa 37

Crabmeat Spread 29

Cranberry Salsa 36

Cranberry-Pineapple Salsa 37

Cucumber Dip 17

Curry Dip for Raw Vegetables 9

Fruit Dip 26
Fruit with Lime Dip 24
Garbanzo Dip 10
Horseradish Dip 16
Hot Crab Dip 2
Hot Pecan Dip 20
Hot Seafood Spread 28
Hummus 29
Jalapeño Cheese Spread 32
King Artichoke Dip 13
Layered Pizza Dip 22
Lobster Dip 6
Louisiana Shrimp Dip 5
Maple Syrup Dip 25
Margarita Jalapeño Salsa 35
Marshmallow Cream Dip 27
Mediterranean Feta Dip 23
Mex-Dip 1
Mexican Corn Dip 14
Nacho Chicken Spread 31
Olive Spread with Walnuts 30
Quick Fruit Dip 24
Raspberry Chipotle Black Bean Dip 11
Reuben Dip 8
Roasted Eggplant and Pesto Spread 31
Roasted Eggplant Dip 17
Roasted Onion Guacamole Dip 15
Rum Fruit Dip 25
Salmon Tartar Spread 30

Sandy's Mushroom Spread 19
Sausage Dip 2
Seafood Salsa 33
Shrimp and Crab Dip 5
Shrimp Dip 3
Shrimp Layered Dip 4
Shrimp Mess 28
Smoked Salmon and Dill Dip 7
Smoky Egg Dip 19
Southern Caviar Dip 18
Spicy Peanut Dip 20
Spinach Artichoke Salsa Dip 18
Strawberry Salsa 36
Sun-Dried Tomato Basil Dip 9
Taco Dip Supreme 1
Three Cheese Baked Artichoke Dip 12
Tropical Fruit Salsa 35
Vegetable Dip 16
Very Gouda Spread 32
White Cheese Dip 22
Yogurt Dip 27
Zerbe's Shrimp Dip 4

VEGETABLE APPETIZERS

Arkansas Caviar 57
Artichoke Cheese Squares 39
Artichoke Cheesecake 40
Artichoke Frittata 41

Artichoke Nibbles 39
Asparagus Rollers 54
Asparagus Wraps 55
Baked Garlic 56
Black Bean Cakes 43
Cajun Stuffed Mushrooms 53
Cheese Balled Olives 43
Cherry Bombs 54
Chipotle Fried Onion Rings 57
Deviled Eggs 46
Fried Jalapeños II 45
Fried Jalapeños 44
Grilled Marinated Mushrooms 53
Gruyere Cheese Stuffed Celery 45
Guacamole Dip 42
Hot Olive Cheese Puffs 44
Italian-Style Quesadillas 41
Marinated Broccoli 58
Marinated Mushrooms and Cheese 50
Marinated Mushrooms 49
Mushroom Pâté 51
Mushroom Puffs 49
Mushrooms Stuffed with Pesto and Cheese 52
Salsa Potato Skins 42
Spinach Balls 47
Spinach Burritos 48
Spinach Mushrooms 50
Spinach Spirals 47
Stuffed Cream Cheese Mushrooms 48

Tex-Mex Deviled Eggs 46
Zucchini French Fries 56
Zucchini Sticks 55

MEAT & POULTRY APPETIZERS

Aramadilla Eggs 72
Bacon and Date Appetizer 72
Baked Chicken Wings 68
Baked Egg Rolls 59
Barbequed Chicken Wings 69
Bite-Size Taco Turnovers 67
Bourbon Chicken 70
Braunschweiger Pate 79
Chinese-Style Barbequed Ribs 77
Cranberry Meatballs 62
Easy as 1-2-3 71
Ham Ball 75
Ham Rolls with Mushrooms 75
Hanky Panks 67
Hot Wings 68
Mandarin Pork Kabobs 78
Marinated Sirloin 66
Mexican Egg Rolls 60
Mini Reubens 78
Mini-Quiches 74
Oriental Meatballs 63
Pepperoni Cheese Munchers 73
Pork Meatballs 64

Quesadilla Meatballs 61
Ranch Meatballs 61
Rib Bites 76
Rumaki 71
Sausage Balls 65
South of the Border Meatballs 62
Super Nachos 66
Swedish Meatballs 63
Sweet and Sour Meatballs 64
Tamale Balls 65
Tex-Mex Chicken Munchies 70
USA Egg Rolls 60

SEAFOOD & FISH APPETIZERS

Cajun Crabmeat Mold 83
Caviar Pie 93
Ceviche 92
Crab and Artichoke Tarts 81
Crab Puff 82
Crab Quiches 83
Crab Roll-Ups with Avocado Dip 84
Dot's Crabbies 81
Hot Crab Muffins 82
Layered Crab Dip 85
Lobster Canapes 90
Party Crabmeat 85
Pickled Shrimp 88
Salmon Ball II 95

Salmon Ball 94
Seafood Tarts 91
Shrimp Nachos 86
Shrimp Paste 89
Shrimp Pate 88
Shrimp Quiches 86
Shrimp Taco 90
Shrimp Toast 89
Smoked Salmon Sushi Roll 94
Smoky Chipotle Trout Pate 95
Sushi Roll 93
Tequila Lime Shrimp 87

CHEESE APPETIZERS

Baked Brie 105
Baked Goat Cheese.. 97
Blue Cheese and Brandy Cheese Ball 114
Blue Cheese Puffs 109
Cheese Roll... 99
Cheese Shorties 104
Chili Cheese Squares 101
Chili Cheesecake 100
Chili Quiche Appetizers 113
Chili-Cheese Balls 114
Chutney Baked Brie 105
Cowboy Crisp 116
Fiesta Brie.. 106
Fiesta Cream Cheese 100

Fried Cheddar Cheese 103
Goat Cheese with Sun-Dried Tomatoes 97
Green Chili Won Tons 108
Holiday Cheese Ball 98
Hot Baked Brie 108
Jalapeño Fudge 110
Jalapeño Squares 101
Mexican Baked Brie 107
Mexican Pinwheels 109
Phyllo Feta Wraps 110
Pimiento Cheese 103
Pineapple Salsa 106
Pita Cheese Crisps 115
Quesadillas with Creamy Salsa 99
Reuben Roll-Ups 102
Roquefort Cheese Ball 98
Roquefort Pecan Log 104
Salsa Cheese Bale 112
Southern Cheese Ball 113
Texas Tortillas 111
Tortilla Roll-Ups 102

FONDUE

Beef Cheese Fondue 119
Caramel-Pecan Fondue 123
Cheese and Wild Mushroom Fondue 122
Cheese Fondue 121
Chili Fondue 119

Chocolate Fondue 124
Flaming Turtle Chocolate Fondue 123
Hot Crab Fondue 120
Lobster Fondue 120
Mexican Fondue 122
Shrimp Fondue 121
Spicy Chicken Fondue 117
Sweet and Sour Fondue 118
Texas Fondue 118

BRUSCHETTA, CHIPS & BREAD

Artichoke Bruschetta 128
B. L. T. Bruschetta 125
Blue Cheese Bruschetta 127
Bruschetta with Fresh Tomatoes and Garlic 126
Bruschetta with Roasted Peppers 126
Cheddar Shortbread 131
Focaccia 131
Mushroom Bruschetta 125
Pita Chips 130
Roquefort Biscuits 130
Seasoned Crackers 132
Spicy Potato Chips 129
Sweet Potato Chips 129
Triscuit Bruschetta 128
Walnut Bruschetta.. 127

MISCELLANEOUS APPETIZERS

Barbeque Pecans 135
Caramel Corn 136
Cream Cheese Strawberries 133
Dog Food 139
Fire Mouth Popcorn 137
Nacho Popcorn 136
Parmesan-Curry Popcorn 137
Ranch Pecans 134
Roquefort Grapes 133
Roquefort Pecans 134
Spicy Pumpkin Seeds 135
Texas Trash 138
White Trash 138

THE COOKBOOK CO.

ANY BITCH CAN COOK

ANY BITCH CAN PARTY

ANY BITCH CAN DRINK

SUGAR BITCHES

ANY BITCH CAN FAKE IT

ANY BITCH CAN SALSA

MERRY BITCHIN HOLIDAYS

EAT BITCH & WINE

ANY QUEEN CAN DECORATE

www.anybitchcookbooks.com